P9-DEG-659

Lucy Crawford's History
of the White Mountains

Lucy Howe Crawford, about 1860

Lucy Crawford's History of the White Mountains

Edited & with an Introduction by

Stearns Morse

Appalachian Mountain Club
Boston, Massachusetts

10 9 8 7

© 1966 by Trustees of Dartmouth College
© 1978 by Appalachian Mountain Club
Library of Congress Catalog Card Number: 66–17763
Title-page wood engraving by John Melanson

CONTENTS

—

CHAPTER I

*First visit to the White Mountains. Names
and heights of the different summits.*   3

CHAPTER II

*Early settlers of Coos County. Their habits,
courage and enterprise.*   9

CHAPTER III

*The Crawfords. Their privations and
hardships. Ethan's marriage.*   25

CHAPTER IV

*Burning of the Crawford House. Sickness
of Mrs. Crawford. Narrow escape from the
flames.*   33

ILLUSTRATIONS

———

iv

PUBLISHER'S PREFACE

T HE Appalachian Mountain Club has been at home in the White Mountains since it was organized more than a century ago. And, it has been concerned about the history of the region—mainly through its journal, *Appalachia*—since the beginning. It is appropriate, then, that it should now be reprinting perhaps the best-loved book on the area—*Lucy Crawford's History of the White Mountains*.

This edition essentially reproduces the work of Dartmouth College professor Stearns Morse, who provided to University Press of New England a collated work based on the first edition of 1846, subsequent editions printed in the late nineteenth-century, and recently rediscovered additional manuscript. (Morse's introduction, which follows, provides a fascinating account of how he edited Lucy's revision of her own book, an unpublished manuscript written in her own hand in 1860, and subsequently given to Dartmouth College by an heir.)

There is one important addition to this new edition, the long-lost plates to which Morse refers in the introduction. Unexpectedly, more of Lucy's manuscript, as well as woodblocks drawn in pencil by Marshall Tidd but never carved, recently came to light. The material was donated to Dartmouth College by William Crawford Wheeler of Bangor, a great, great grandson of Ethan Allen and Lucy Crawford.

Included here are the nine woodblocks recovered. A tenth, a portrait mentioned by Tidd elsewhere, was probably not done; Tidd noted that another artist would have to do it since portraits were not his line.

ARLYN S. POWELL, JR.
DIRECTOR OF PUBLICATIONS
APPALACHIAN MOUNTAIN CLUB

ACKNOWLEDGMENTS

I HAVE already recorded in the introduction my gratitude to Mrs. Helen Crawford Wells for her invaluable assistance. I should like to add here my thanks to Mrs. Dorothy H. Willson, Town Clerk of Lancaster, New Hampshire, for putting me in touch with Mrs. Wells. My thanks, too, to Mrs. Marion B. Powers, Town Clerk of Lunenburg, Vermont, for passing on to me useful information about the Rosebrook and Howe families compiled by the late Eldon B. Hartshorn. My indebtedness to Frederick W. Kilbourne's *Chronicles of the White Mountains* and to F. Allen Burt's *The Story of Mount Washington* has been indicated in the notes. I should like to thank also: my fellow townsman, Albert Rosebrook, for lending me a genealogy of the Rosebrook family compiled by Marion Rosebrook Emmons; Mrs. Elizabeth Sherrard of the Rare Books Department of the Baker Library of Dartmouth College for help with the illustrations; and my wife for preparing the index.

Additional thanks are due Nanine Hutchinson of the University Press of New England for caring enough to find a new home for the book; Walter Wright of Dartmouth College for his help with the illustrations; William Crawford Wheeler for donating the illustrations to Dartmouth; and, Hank Bennett of Book Press for his care in reprinting the book.

FOREWORD

———

THERE is no more beautiful region in the United States than northern Vermont and New Hampshire with their hills and mountains, fertile valleys, and many lakes and streams. My father was born in northern Vermont in the town of Guildhall on the Connecticut river, in the Old Home Crawford where his father and grandfather lived before him. His happy boyhood on this typical New England farm filled him with memories that remained vivid through his long life. Though he left the Old Home Crawford at the age of fifteen to live with an uncle near Boston in order to receive a college education, he never lost his intense love of his homeland.

Later, as children came along, Father delighted in telling us tales of the North Country: of Rogers Rangers, of Indians, of the struggles of early settlers. A favorite tale was the story of Uncle Abel Crawford, a giant of a man, farmer, trapper, mountaineer, who moved east in his quest for elbow room till he settled in the great notch in the mountains which now bears his name. Uncle Abel cut the bridle path up Mount Washington, became a guide for scientists and mountain climbers who desired to scale this dangerous mountain. He became a sort of patriarch of the mountains and patron saint of American mountain climbers.

His son Ethan Allen Crawford, also a tall and powerful pioneer, settled near the Notch and carried on the work of his father. In 1803 the wagon road through the Notch was built, shortening the distance from Portland, Maine to the

new settlements above the mountains. Long wagon trains
began to arrive at Ethan's farm, bringing supplies to the
North Country settlers. After the long steep climb through
the mountains, rest and food were necessary for horses
and men. Thus Ethan's farm became an inn. This was the
beginning of the hotels of future years—Fabyans, on the
site of Ethan's farm, and four miles east at the head of the
Notch, the famous Crawford House.

Ethan's wife Lucy, a woman of some education, shared
the rugged hardships of these pioneering years. In later
life she wrote the story of her experiences and called it *The
History of the White Mountains.* It was pretty much a biography of her father-in-law, Abel Crawford, and her husband, Ethan Allen Crawford. A limited edition of this
little book appeared in 1846. In 1883, thirteen years after
her death, a second edition was printed in limited numbers; in 1886 there was a reprint of this edition: all three
editions have long been out of print.

After my father retired from business he spent many
happy summers in the Old Home Crawford in Guildhall.
During this time he found much pleasure in researching
Crawford family history. He wrote several books, among
them a biography of his father, Oramel Crawford, born at
the old home in 1809. The life of Ethan Allen Crawford
always interested Father, and in his ninety-third year he
began to accumulate material for a biography of Ethan
Allen Crawford. Unfortunately, Father did not live to ac-
complish this ambition.

Some years later a manuscript written by Lucy Crawford came into my possession. Apparently, Lucy, in her
old age, was not satisfied with her history and desired to
publish a new edition, including corrections and new
material. Friends urged me to have this manuscript edited

and published. What finer tribute could there be to both my father and to Lucy Crawford?

Professor Stearns Morse of Dartmouth College has consented to edit the manuscript and prepare it for publication. Professor Morse, himself a native of New Hampshire, now spending his summers on his ancestral farm near the little village of Swiftwater (What lovelier name could a New Hampshire village have?), has already coauthored a book about the White Mountains, and has wide knowledge of the early history of New England.

I hope readers of this little book will receive as much pleasure from it as we have in planning its publication.

FREDERICK C. CRAWFORD

INTRODUCTION

LUCY CRAWFORD'S *History* has the place of honor as the first of the classics in Bent's *Bibliography of the White Mountains*. Before the publication of her book in 1846 many incidental references to the White Mountains had been printed in books and journals, notably in Governor Winthrop's *Journal*, published in 1790, which contains the first printed account of the first ascent of Mount Washington by Darby Field in 1642; in Volume 3 (published in 1792) of Jeremy Belknap's *History of New Hampshire:* and in Volume 2 (published in 1821) of Timothy Dwight's *Travels in New England and New York*. Since her book there has been, of course, a flood of books and articles: Bent, in the introduction to his bibliography, published in 1911, observes that the White Mountains "have had more written about them, probably, than any other mountains, the Alps alone excepted"—perhaps the Himalayas should be another exception.

The first edition was a small book; the publisher's imprint was "The White Hills"; it was printed by F. A. & A. F. Gerrish, No. 74, Middle Street, Portland. In 1883 a second edition was published, with a preface by Henry Wheelock Ripley; the publisher was Hoyt, Fogg & Donham, of Portland. This had a portrait of Abel Crawford as a frontispiece. It was reprinted in 1886, from the same plates. This reprint was put out by B. Thurston & Co. of Portland, which had printed the 1883 edition. Both of these editions contained supplementary material: The White Mountains, Where to Go and What to See; engrav-

ings of mountain scenes; advertisements of mountain hos-
telries; etc.

The *History* is not only a White Mountains classic, it is
a classic of Americana. For it gives not only an account of
the visits of travellers to the Presidential Range in the
first half of the century; it is also a vivid account of a pioneer family, their trials, perils and adventures in settling
in the wilderness; of the famous Crawford hostelry, which
came to be known as Crawford's Old Moosehorn Tavern,
with its famous guests—William Oakes, the botanist;
Daniel Webster; Emerson and Hawthorne (though Lucy
does not mention them in the *History*); and of two epic
characters, Abel Crawford, the "Patriarch", and his son,
Ethan Allen, "the mountain giant"; not to mention perhaps the most intrepid character of them all, Lucy herself.

In present-day fashion, I suppose, the authorship could
be given as "Ethan Allen Crawford, as told to Lucy, his
wife" for the narrative is in the first person. And in Chapter X Ethan gives an account of how the book came to be
written. Lucy had kept a record, "for there seemed to be
something very extraordinary in our affairs in life, which
was an inducement for her labor . . . in order to be able to
show the public our way of trying to get a living, by dealing honestly with men, and having a clear conscience as
regards my management with mankind." Moreover there
was a financial inducement: if they could publish and sell
the history "it would be an assistance" to regaining their
farm in Guildhall. "She found time": the book was written; copyrighted in 1845 and published in 1846; but by
then "the mountain giant" was dead. Lucy survived her
husband for twenty-three years and died, at the age of
seventy-six, in 1869.

Nine years before that date five other White Mountains

"classics" had been published: William Oakes's *Scenery of the White Mountains* in 1848; John H. Spaulding's *Historical Relics of the White Mountains* in 1855; an account of the "perilous adventures" of Dr. B. L. Ball on Mount Washington, "written by himself" in 1856; *Incidents in White Mountain History*, by Benjamin G. Willey in 1856; and Starr King's *The White Hills* in 1860. It was partly this growing interest in the White Mountains region which led Lucy Crawford to revise her original work and to apply for a copyright in 1860.

The manuscript begins with a notice

To the Public

In 1846 the author of the following pages published a small work entitled "The History of the White Mountains" but through the carelessness of the printer and the Crawford family leaving the Mountains about that time a second edition was never issued.

Since the above period other works relative to the "White Hills" have been presented to the public, but the connection by marriage of the author of this work to one of the earliest settlers and her long residence at the mountains gives her advantage for narrating facts concerning the hardships of the first emigrants to this romantic spot.

The great slide of 1826 as well as the biography of the Crawford family [can be told] more correctly than can be given by any other person.

Her knowledge of the above facts and the great changes that have taken place about those regions since 1846 has induced her to revise and enlarge her former work not only that the public may be correctly informed of the hardships and privations to which those hardy mountaineers were subjected, but also to aid the writer in her declining years to regain her old homestead.

Literary fame is no part of our intention. We leave that to those, whose imagination serves them as a guide rather than facts, while we speak of circumstances coming under our own observation, and from early history.

Considerable expense has attended this book in furnishing plates, representing some of the most noted localities, as well as some of the feats of the mountain giant.

After her death the first thirteen chapters of the manuscript apparently came into the possession of her daughter, Ellen Wile Howard. From Stoneham, Massachusetts she mailed it on August 13, 1908 to her nephew, Ethan Allen Crawford III, at Jefferson Highlands, New Hampshire, who left it to his daughter, Mrs. Lucy Howe Crawford Merrill. On February 23, 1951 she sent it to the Crawford House, suggesting in a letter that it might be put on sale. That fall it was acquired by Mr. Frederick C. Crawford of Cleveland, Ohio and Guildhall, Vermont, who is sponsoring the present publication. In the letter offering the manuscript for sale, Mrs. Merrill—Lucy's great-granddaughter—wrote: "Most of the book was written by Lucy—I do not know who wrote the rest of it, probably one of her children. The spicier passages were cut out by her daughter, Lucy, who was an ardent member of the WCTU, and intended to see that no mention was made of Ethan's occasional lapses from virtue." She also says that around 1902, John Anderson, the manager for Joseph Stickney, owner of the Mount Pleasant House and the Mount Washington Hotel at Bretton Woods, suggested to her great aunts that they publish the manuscript, but nothing came of it.

Though Lucy Crawford applied for copyright in 1860 with the hope of publication, we do not know what measures she took, if any, to get her manuscript published. It appears likely that she worked on the manuscript during subsequent years. Chapter XIII, the reader will note, is chiefly devoted to an account of the towns around the mountains. The manuscript ends rather abruptly with a brief paragraph about Conway "at the present day", that is, 1860 or thereabouts. F. Allen Burt in his *Story of Mount Washington* quotes an account of her husband's death which does not appear in the manuscript of the first thirteen chapters. Mr. Burt ascribed this description, in a note, to an "unpublished manuscript intended as a closing chapter to her *History of the White Mountains*, formerly in the possession of her granddaughter, the late Hattie B. Crawford of Lancaster, N. H."

Several inquiries about Lucy Crawford's life after the death of her husband had been fruitless, but following this clue I wrote to the town clerk of Lancaster to ask if there was any information about the Crawford family in the town records. She referred me to Mrs. Helen Crawford Wells of Shelburne Falls, Massachusetts, Lucy's great-granddaughter. There ensued a lively correspondence with Mrs. Wells and finally a visit to her from which I returned bearing not only the missing final chapter but also several pictures including the photograph of Lucy Crawford which is the frontispiece of this edition. For these treasures as well as for her reminiscences of her family it is appropriate here to record our great gratitude to Mrs. Wells.

It is apparent from Chapter I, which consists of material not in the published book, that it was Lucy's intention in her revision to write a book about the mountains rather than about the Crawford family: a commendable desire, to achieve some sort of unity, except that, unfortunately, it makes for a duller and less personal narrative. We should be grateful, therefore, that in this final chapter Lucy departed from her original intention. She elaborates the account of Ethan Allen Crawford's illness given in Chapter X, is more explicit about the "premature decay

xviii INTRODUCTION

of his mind". And she goes into greater detail as to the events that led to the final loss of their homestead. She leaves us in no doubt as to the sharp practices of the Messrs. Abbott *et al.* But her complaints of their chicanery seem under the circumstances, dignified and without venom; nor does she spare herself reproaches for her trustfulness in signing the deed without full realization of what she might be doing. Naturally, of course, she gives us the Crawford side of this rather involved transaction, but this should not prevent us from sharing with her the pathos of their loss of the old home as she describes it.

Moving, too, is her simple account of the final destruction by fire of the place that had meant so much to her and to Ethan, the place where they had suffered hardship and privation, but where also they had triumphed over their adversities and won enviable reputations as the master and the mistress of the famous mountain hostelry. The account of this catastrophe, too, is quite without sentimentality—

> One had to be versed in country things
> Not to believe the phoebes wept.

The tone of this last chapter is somewhat mournful and nostalgic; this is natural for an old woman looking back on an exciting and eventful past. But it is also good to know that her last days were spent with her children. We are grateful for the account of her daughters' venture in the Lowell boarding house, the Lowell of Lucy Larcom, Whittier and *The Lowell Offering*. This is a pleasant reminder of the days when North Country girls went down to work in the mills to earn a competence before marriage; to enjoy, as Lucy puts it, "a pleasant employment" and hours of leisure spent in improvement of the mind.

Abel Crawford, from a painting by Chester Harding, 1846

The Willey House in Crawford Notch, from a photograph taken in 1875 by Fred E. Crawford. The old house at the right is the one which escaped the slide of 1826

The Mount Crawford House and Mount Crawford, from a photograph taken in 1875 by Fred E. Crawford

Nor did this urban experience of her daughters appear to weaken their Crawford fibre. For two of them, then married and living in New Hampshire, were the first women to make a winter ascent of Mount Washington. With a brother and a nephew they left Jefferson at eight o'clock on the morning of February 24, 1874; rode the nineteen miles to the camp of their brother, Ethan Allen Crawford II, at the base of the mountain (though he was absent); started up the railroad at 2 p.m. and arrived at the summit at five, their faces "slightly frozen, the wind blowing 50 miles per hour, with the thermometer 8 degrees below zero." Three gentlemen of the U. S. Signal Service instantly applied cold water to the frozen faces and provided an ample repast "in Parker House style". The newspaper account concludes:

> Aside from a little natural fatigue, these descendants of Old Ethan, the Pioneer, experienced no more inconvenience from their hazardous enterprise, than did their ancestor in his accustomed labor scaling the pathless crags of the same mountain.

But to return to Lucy and her *History*. At the end of the edition of 1846 there is a page of errata—they were corrected in the edition of 1883—followed by this statement:

> There are numerous errors, grammatical and typographical, still uncorrected, which the reader will please rectify. The disadvantages under which the work went to press—illegible manuscript—want of time—the proof sheets not having been read by the author, &c., &c., will, we trust, be a sufficient reason for the manner in which it appears before the public.

Since the book was being printed around the time of Ethan's illness and death the "disadvantages" are understandable. The reference to illegible manuscript is rather puzzling for the manuscript of 1860 is eminently legible— it was probably written at a more leisurely pace. The man-

uscript is in two different handwritings; here and there—
this is especially true of Chapter XIV—it appears to be in
a third hand. One handwriting is somewhat crabbed, evidently formed before the influence of P. R. Spencer had
begun to take effect: this is probably Lucy's. The other
hands are a flowing Spencerian script and are probably her
daughters'. But all three hands are clear and firm.

In both the 1846 and the 1883 editions Chapter I is
headed "The Rosebrooks", Chapter II "The Crawfords".
After that there are no chapter headings. The edition of
1883, however, has a table of contents: in this Chapters III
to IX inclusive are given the title "Reminiscences"; Chapter X is entitled "Reminiscences, Improvements and
Weather". In the manuscript of 1860 Lucy has headed each
chapter as given in the "Contents" (which she called the
"Index"). In order, therefore, to make the substance of
each chapter correspond to the indicated contents I have
followed the chapter arrangement of the manuscript rather
than of the book. (It will be noted that her "contents" are
not always complete—as in Chapters IV and X, for example.)

I have mentioned the fact that Chapter I of the manuscript consists of material not in the book; this is also true
of Chapters XI, XII and most of Chapter XIII—a few pages
of this chapter she lifted from Chapter X of the book.
(None of Chapter XIV, of course, was in the book.) With
these exceptions she followed closely the printed volume
of 1846. In a few places passages are transposed, but for
the most part she follows the order of the book; some of
the book is paraphrased, much of it is taken over verbatim; in several places she has cut passages from the book
and pasted them into the manuscript.

There are, however, two important differences between

the manuscript and the book. The manuscript is considerably abridged—the book is almost twice as long. The reason for this abridgement is clear from what I have said of the nature of Chapter I—that is, Lucy's intention to concentrate on the mountains rather than on her family. The other important difference is that the manuscript is in the third person: Mr. Crawford or Ethan or "the mountain giant" did thus and so. This, too, makes for a much less vivid, vigorous and colorful performance than the first person narrative of the book.

In spite of her disclaimer of a desire for "literary fame" I have a sneaking suspicion that Lucy, with the example of her contemporary White Mountains authors in mind, was bitten by the notion of prettifying her original document somewhat. Her two poems in the last chapter—to say nothing of the religious sentiments expressed—indicate a somewhat self-conscious "literary" bent. Revisions are not always improvements. Were it not for the additional information we glean about her family Lucy's manuscript of 1860 by itself would not be especially interesting except as a curiosity. Hence the reason for reprinting the book, with such additions from the manuscript as seem relevant.

To repeat, Chapters I, XI, XII, most of Chapter XIII, and Chapter XIV are fresh material. In the rest of the text I have inserted passages from the manuscript in brackets where they do not seriously interrupt or impede the flow of the narrative. I have relegated to the notes interesting variations or revisions; these passages I have transcribed verbatim, Lucy's mistakes, occasional grammatical lapses and all. Nor have I tampered much with Lucy's writing in the body of the text.

On page 18 Ethan comments on "the want of good schools" for his grandmother Rosebrook's children.

"But," he says, "as their mother had in early life acquired a knowledge of letters and the proper use of them, she instructed them so well that they could read and spell with considerable accuracy." Grandmother Rosebrook was also Lucy's grandmother, and her literacy was obviously passed on to the second generation. Though she could have had only a common school education, her writing, I think, will stand comparison with that of most college freshmen today. Her spelling certainly will stand such a comparison: wherever she misspells it is almost always a slip of the pen, so that I have not hesitated occasionally to correct a misspelling—she would have done it herself, I am sure, if she had time to prepare her manuscript for the press. I have retained her spelling of geographical names: Amanoosuc, for instance, and Winnepiseogee. Her paragraphing, both in the manuscript and the book, is sometimes erratic, but I have for the most part left it alone. In general she knows how to punctuate: she is especially adept in the use of the semicolon. She was overly fond of commas, and I have surreptitiously eliminated some of them, but not always consistently.

In short, I have great respect for her as a writer. Nor have I intended to be patronizing about any literary aspirations she may have secretly cherished. The poems of her last chapter may not be great poetry, but one has certainly read worse. At least they are spontaneous expressions of a genuine emotion for the place where she spent her happiest years. And such a phrase as "the new slain woodland", for instance, reveals a poetic sensitivity such as one often finds in people who have observed nature directly rather than through books. One thing her writing succeeds in achieving, as any good writing should: it beautifully gives you an idea of the sort of person she was.

And I think she was admirable—and her mountain giant, too.

But where are the plates to which she went to considerable expense to furnish the book with representations of "the most noted localities, as well as some of the feats of the mountain giant"? Alas, they seem to have vanished. For them I have substituted some of the material appended to the edition of 1883 (even though there is some repetition of the text); a few of the advertisements of transportation (so far as railroads go, superior to that of today) and of mountain hotels; and a map of the Crawford Country. With these and with Lucy's book and her revisions in hand the reader may be able to recreate in his imagination the White Mountains wilderness of the pioneers and the summer hotel life of the 1880's, scarcely less remote from the superhighways of today.

STEARNS MORSE

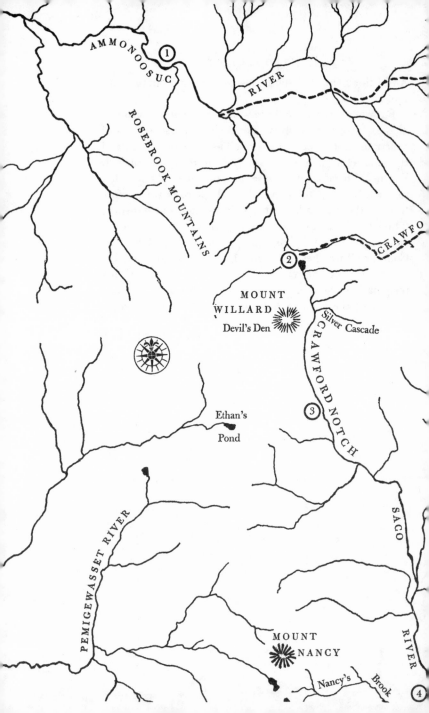

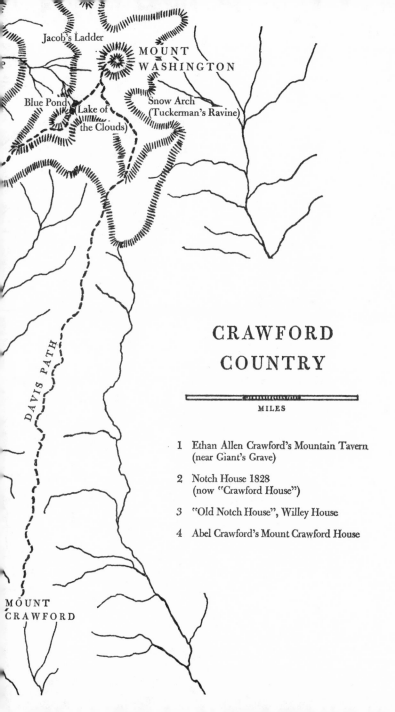

Jacob's Ladder

MOUNT
WASHINGTON

Blue Pond
Lake of
the Clouds

Snow Arch
(Tuckerman's Ravine)

DAVIS PATH

CRAWFORD
COUNTRY

MILES

1 Ethan Allen Crawford's Mountain Tavern
(near Giant's Grave)

2 Notch House 1828
(now "Crawford House")

3 "Old Notch House", Willey House

4 Abel Crawford's Mount Crawford House

MOUNT
CRAWFORD

Lucy Crawford's History
of the White Mountains

INTRODUCTION

——

IT may be inquired by some persons, what has become of Crawford, the mountaineer, or Ethan of the hills. It will be the endeavor of the authoress of this tale to relate some of his misfortunes and adventures, briefly as possible, it being always a rule with him to make short stories and not go a great way round to effect a small thing.

This she has done, in his own language, as nearly as she could, for the information of others and the benefit of all of her own family whom she is desirous of bringing up and making useful members of society. These are all true statements of things which have taken place within her own knowledge, since she has been living with him. These facts he was unwilling at first to have published, as he did not wish to expose those who seemed to be against him. They have been stated in as moderate terms as possible, as we do not wish to injure the feelings even of enemies if we have any such. It will readily be seen why he was always involved in debt, if this history is read with candor and viewed in a right manner, as it will show his misfortunes to have originated, first, in the fire, which left him a large sum in debt; next, in being obliged to build almost every year, so far from common privileges; and then, in the two freshets, which caused him a heavy loss of property. Taking all these things into consideration, it may be wondered how he succeeded in getting along as well as he did, under so many losses and disappointments. But, saith the poet:

> Pigmies placed on alps, are pigmies still;
> And pyramids are pyramids in vales.

And, as the scriptures saith of men of ancient times:

> There were giants in those days.

CHAPTER I

—

First visit to the White Mountains.
Names and heights of the
different summits.

AGIOCHOOK, the aboriginal name of the White
Mountains, appears by history to have been an object
of interest to some as early as 1642. Dr. Belknap, in his
history of New Hampshire, relates an account of their
being visited during the summer season of the above year,
twice, by one Darby Field, who lived about Piscataquack.
He was accompanied in his first excursion by two Indians.
Near the foot of the Mountains, at the head of the Saco
river, he came to an Indian town of some 200 inhabitants.
Some of them ascended within about eight miles of the
top with Field, but would not proceed any further from
some superstitious ideas they entertained. They tried to
dissuade Mr. Field from going further, telling him no
Indian ever durst venture any higher, and that he would
die if he went. In Mr. Field's description of the Mountains,
he says, "They went divers times through thick clouds,
for a good space, and within four miles of the top they had
no clouds, but very cold." The thousands who have visited
Mount Washington since that time can well vouch for the
correctness of his statement.

Mr. Field made his second visit about one month after
his first. He was accompanied this time by five or six persons. This company brought away some stones which they

3

supposed to be diamond but which proved to be crystal. This gave rise to the name of "Crystal Hills." It has been supposed by some, from the description which Field gave of his ascension, that he went up the mountain near "Tuckerman's Ravine." Time has somewhat changed the facilities since the period of Field's day, as it took him about eighteen days to perform the journey. Some statements made by him appear to be very incorrect. He says (according to Governor Winthrop's account) that "the distance from Saco is about 100 miles; that after 40 miles travel, he did, for the most part ascend, and within 12 miles of the top was neither tree nor grass, but low savins, which they went upon the top of sometimes." His ideas of distance appear to be wild. Twelve miles is the extent of either of the Mountain Houses of the present day, and nearly one-half of that distance is through a *forest*. At some former period vegetation has flourished much higher up the mountain than at the present time. Within two or three miles of the summit may be seen large clusters of dwarf trees without any foliage. By some it is supposed that life was taken from them by the extreme cold weather of former years. Soon after the visits of Field to the White Hills, Messrs. Vines and Gorges, two of the magistrates of Sir F. Gorges' province, made the ascent. Their description, as well as that of others of later date, seems somewhat exaggerated, owing undoubtedly to their professing no knowledge of the surrounding country, and beating about over a large territory without a guide or landmarks, as at the present day.

Perhaps no range of mountains in the world presents a greater variety of scenery than the White Mountains. Ascend either of the peaks forming this chain of hills, and each and every view produces a feeling of admiration to all lovers of the works of nature. Such sublimity as the eye beholds at almost every step tends to encourage the tourist over the ragged cliffs, forgetting the fatigue he has experienced in anticipation of a rich feast when seated upon the summit.

In 1820, seven persons, consisting of Adino N. Brackett, John W. Weeks, General John Willson, Charles J. Stuart, N. S. Dennison and Samuel A. Pearsons of Lancaster, and Philip Carrigan (author of Carrigan's Map of New Hampshire), with Ethan A. Crawford as guide, ascended Mount Washington for the purpose of giving a name to each of the several peaks.[1] The following are the names and their respective heights.

Mount Washington standing nearly in the center of the chain, is 6,285 feet. To the north, Mount Clay next appears, 5,011 feet; Mount Adams, third to the north, is 5,790 feet; Mount Jefferson, 5,710 feet; Mount Madison, 5,361. To the south of Mount Washington, Munroe, first in order, is 5,349 feet; Franklin, 4,850 feet; Mount Pleasant, 4,715 feet; Clinton, 4,200. This comprises the principal chain on the northerly side of the Notch. Upon the southerly side of the pass through the Notch, another chain reaches from Bartlett through to the Franconia notch, forming a range of less magnitude than the one on the northerly side.

[At this point half a page has been cut from Lucy Crawford's manuscript and a passage inserted in another hand. Except for the introductory phrase, "As Ethan says", this passage is taken practically verbatim from Chapter IV of the printed book and since the changes are slight and probably due to carelessness in copying I have followed the text of the book.]

[As Ethan says] we rode to the Notch, and there I was

loaded equal to a pack-horse, with cloaks and necessary articles for two nights, with a plenty of what some call "Black Betts," or "O-be-joyful," as it was the fashion in those days, to make use of this kind of stuff, and especially upon such occasions. We traveled on until we reached the camp, about three miles from the road, then I struck up a fire, cut wood, and prepared our usual supper, spread our blankets, brought for that purpose, and after some interesting stories told by the party, I believe we all fell asleep. In the morning, after breakfast, we started on our intended expedition, taking only provisions enough for the day, and a sufficient quantity of "O-be-joyful," and set forward and went over several hills, and came to a beautiful pond of clear water, distant one mile from the apex of the hill. Here we made a stop for some time, enjoying the water, which was delicious, and then went to the summit of Mount Washington. There they gave names to several peaks, and then drank healths to them in honor to the great men whose names they bore, and gave toasts to them; and after they had all got through, they put it upon me to do the same; but as this was a new thing to me, and not being prepared, I could only express my feelings by saying I hoped all of us might have good success and return to our respective families in safety, and find them in health; which was answered by a cheer from all, as they had cheered at other times before, when any one had drank a toast. The day was fine, and our feelings seemed to correspond with the beauties of the day, and after some hours had swiftly passed away in this manner, we concluded to leave this grand and magnificent place and return to a lower situation on earth. We then left the hill, and came down to the before mentioned pond. Here we staid a long time partaking of its waters, until some of us became quite blue, and from this circumstance we agreed to give it the name of Blue Pond,[2] and at rather a late hour we left it and proceeded toward the camp, but did not all arrive there until nine o'clock in the evening. This water so much troubled one of our party, or the elevated situation on which we traveled, fatigue, or some other cause, had such an effect upon him that he could not get along without my assistance; and he being a man of two hundred weight, caused me to make use of all my strength, at times. I, however, managed to get down at last, and when I did, I was so tired, I prostrated myself upon the ground and told them I could do no more that night, they must look out for themselves, for I was tired to the very bone. They cut some wood and did the best they could that night, and in the morning, sleep had again restored us, so that after taking some refreshment, we started for home, where we all arrived in safety, and in good spirits. Here we with pleasure recalled the proceedings of the previous day, and partaking of another dinner, most of them returned to their places of residence the same day.

[Lucy Crawford's manuscript continues:]

There are at the present day three routes to the top of Mount Washington: one from the Glen House on the northeasterly side, another from the Notch House, the third from the White Mountain House or the old Rosebrook stand. The scenery over these different routes is very unlike. From the Glen but little is to be seen of the surrounding country, a distance of nearly four miles, or until you arrive about one-half the distance up the mountain, the road passing up through a ravine lined upon both sides by a dense forest.

The Notch House road, passing as it does over the tops of several mountains, gives a more extensive view than either of the other two routes, although it is a longer road. From the White Mountain House the road leaves the old turnpike, following along the meadows of the Amonoosuc until it reaches the base of the mountain. The ascent is then rapid and tiresome, but the traveler can find enough to feast the eye while stopping to rest his weary limbs.

To possess a knowledge of the mountains and their beauties, the tourist should pass over each route. It will be noticed by the observing that vegetation extends higher on the western sides of these hills than on the eastern.

CHAPTER II[1]

———

*Early settlers of Coos County.
Their habits, courage
and enterprise.*

HANNAH HANES was born in Brimfield, Massachusetts, August 3, 1744, and at an early age she experienced religion, at the age of seventeen, I think she told me; and this religion supported her through many trying scenes of life; neither did it forsake her in the time of death.

Eleazer Rosebrook was born in Grafton, Massachusetts, 1747; was married to Hannah Hanes, in March, 1772, and there they lived until after the birth of their first child, a daughter; and when this child was one year and a half old, he, like many other enterprising men, took his wife and child and came into what was then called Upper Coos (pronounced Quos), as far as Lancaster. Here they made a temporary stay, while he could look about and find a place to settle, until after the birth of their second child, a daughter. They then moved into the woods, up the Connecticut river as far as Monadnuc or Monadnock, now incorporated as Colebrook, nearly thirty miles from any inhabitant, and without a road. They took the river, in some places, for a guide; and in other places, they followed by marks of spotted trees, which were spotted for the purpose of shortening the distance, and then went into a little log cabin which had been previously prepared by Mr. Rosebrook, my grandfather.

9

Now, in the woods, making a beginning, setting an example for others to follow, suffering many hardships, and enduring many privations common to beginners in a new country, they did the best they could and tried to be content with their situation. They had provided themselves with a cow, the only favored domestic animal they possessed, and, having no pasture, or fence, she was at liberty to range about and go wherever she pleased. Many times did Mrs. Rosebrook, my grandmother, in the absence of her husband, shut her dear child up in her cabin and taking her infant in her arms, proceed into the woods in search of her cow, which she would be directed to find by the sound of her bell. Sometimes she was under the necessity of wading the river to get where the animal was, and then she would return home and find the deserted child safe, and, with the infant still in her arms, and followed by the other child, did she milk her cow, [a prayer of thankfulness offered to Him who "suffereth not a sparrow to fall to the ground." For his protection was over her and her infant children.] What courage must this woman have possessed, after being for many years among near relatives, such as parents, brothers, sisters, and a numerous circle of friends and neighbors, who were near and dear to her, and changing them for the woods! What a contrast between having a large society and now being confined entirely to these her lisping children! What woman in these days could do this and not complain of its being hard or severe? But she had made up her mind to be content and industrious in whatsoever situation she should be placed, and having a monitor within, which would say to her that although separated from earthly friends, yet she had one that would "stick closer than a brother," and while filled with these thoughts, her fears of wild beasts, and many other things, would flee from her. [What a noble example to that class of would be ladies at the present day whose daily labor is performed in brushing the sidewalks with their silks and seek a home when they cannot find any other place of resort.][2]

Their living was principally upon animal food; as God always provides suitably for every one who depends upon him and will apply himself industriously to obtain.

The woods were beautiful and well stored with game, such as moose, deer, bears, etc., and hunters might, in a short time, kill and procure a sufficient quantity of this kind of food to supply their families a long time. Some of the flesh they would dry, and some they would smoke; and, in various ways, did they preserve it and make good wholesome food of it.

One grand article wanted now was salt, which was scarce and hard to be got, and they could not well live without it in this fresh and mountainous country. Some families suffered considerably, by their children having their necks swollen; the disorder was attributed to the want of salt, which was afterward remedied, in a measure, by carrying them to the salt water, and giving them a plenty of salt fish to eat, and applying the skin of the salt fish to their necks; but they never wholly outgrew this trouble. I have heard my grandfather say, that while living in Monadnock, at one time he went on foot to Haverhill and bought one bushel of salt and carried it home through the woods, on his back, a distance, at that time, as they followed the river the most of the way, of not less than eighty miles. Can this same country produce a man now with such wonderful power of muscle and strength of mind to endure this and not complain of its being hard? But such was the courage of these hardy new beginners that they did not mind trifles. One circumstance I think worth recording.

One Major Whitcomb, who lived in this country, went on foot to what was then called Lower Coos, a distance of fifty miles from where he lived, and it was late in the spring; as the people had planted in that place, he had great difficulty in finding potatoes, which it was his whole business to obtain; but he at length succeeded in getting one bushel of small ones, and these he carefully carried home on his back. Those which would answer to cut, he cut in pieces and then planted them. Afterward he counted the hills, and there were four hundred hills of these planted potatoes; and, in the fall, he harvested them and had one hundred bushels of good potatoes. Such was the plentiful increase of almost everything put into the ground. So much so, that this country was considered by people, two or three hundred miles distant, to be equal to the western country now; and those who left their friends to come to this Upper Coos (as they then termed it), were generally a robust and self-denying people; and the friends whom they left behind thought much more of the distance than we do now of going two or three thousand miles; and their expectations of seeing them again were much less than now; which may well be imagined, when we reflect that it is more practicable to travel ten miles now than it was to travel one then. [It required toil and labor to cut down the sturdy forest and prepare the soil with the few implements they possessed. It also required energetic and robust people to undertake the performance of the tasks spoken of above. It did not answer to "put the hand to the plow and look back."]

About this time the Revolutionary War between the United States and Great Britain [was proclaimed and, natural to suppose, the life of the backwoodsman produced courage and a spirit which fitted him to stand up before the enemy and dare to maintain that right which by God's law belonged to him, Liberty.] Grandfather volunteered his services, as he possessed the same independent spirit as our forefathers, and was determined as they were to free our country or shed his own blood in its defense. Before he started, fearing for the safety of his family should he leave them alone, lest they might be destroyed by the enemy, he removed them down to Northumberland, and placed them in a sort of fort, which was then erected and guarded by the husbandmen; they then embraced each other, and he took his leave of his family, having a firm belief that if he had entered rightly into a good cause, he should be prospered, and impressed with these feelings they separated, while his wife's prayers were constantly for him and the general good of the country. But here, in this situation, she did not remain long, having then the addition of another child, a son. A gentleman by the name of White kindly gave her an asylum in his house. As his wife was sickly, and not able to work, he gave her and her three children their board for what they could do; which she considered a great kindness, as it gave her the privilege of supporting herself and family without being chargeable to her husband.

Mrs. Rosebrook remained where she was, on permission, until her husband came home. He then moved his family to Guildhall, Vermont, and having settled them there, returned to his duty for a number of months, discharging it with bravery, and encountering his foes, whenever he was called upon, like a brave soldier.

He and an officer were once sent to Canada as spies. They were suspected, and finding it out, they made good their retreat; they were closely pursued by the enemy. Grandfather was aware of it, and they traveled night as well as day until they came to a considerable stream of water; here they built a fire, and then put it out, to make it appear as though they had been gone for some time; they then waded the stream, and, when at a proper distance, struck up another fire and dried and rested themselves. The enemy came soon after, and found where they had made the fire, which they had extinguished, and, supposing they were out of their reach, returned; as one of the pursuing party told him afterward; and he likewise said that he told them it was useless to follow further, as Mr. Rosebrook was a hunter and a woodsman and knew better than to suffer himself to be overtaken.

Grandmother, while living in Guildhall, in the absence of her husband, was frequently visited by the Indians. As she was a woman and alone, they seemed to make her habitation their place of resort, there being no man to resist them. By disposing of their furs, they would provide themselves with a plenty of what they called uncupy,[3] or spirit, which they carried in bladders taken from moose, and, at times, they would have a great drunk. This troubled her much, knowing their savage dispositions; she, fearing she would offend them and incur their displeasure, bore with them; at one time, however, she became decided and cleared her house of them, all but one, and she was so far gone under the influence of the spirit, or liquor, that she lay motionless upon the floor; grandmother took her by the hair of her head, and with the strength of her feelings, dragged her out of doors; and the squaw by being put in motion, came to herself so much that she had the use of her limbs; she drew her tomahawk and aimed it at Grandmother, who had just closed the door after her, when this tomahawk came so near as to take off the wooden thumb-piece from the door handle; thus she providentially made her escape. Some time in the night, the squaw so far recovered as to move herself out of sight of the house; and the next day, after getting sober and recollecting how ridiculously she had appeared, and what trouble she had caused the good woman the evening before, came back and freely asked her forgiveness, and likewise said she would not do the like again; and she strictly kept her word.

Grandfather came home again, on permission, and as his wife had so much trouble with the natives, and her family being again increased, she did not well know how to have him return; and as he had enlisted during the war, he hired a man to take his place, and remained at home to assist his helpmate in bringing up her young family. As they had begun to fulfil the commandment which was given to Adam at the beginning, it became necessary she should have help; and as a reward for his toils and hardships during his services, he was paid off in old Continental money, which proved a nuisance to him. I have now some of it still in my possession, which I keep in remembrance of his courage and valor.

Peace was proclaimed, and they remained in Guildhall, and the people were, for a number of miles, seemingly all of one family, sharing in each other's bounties and enjoying one another's company, like so many brothers, and if one happened to get a dainty, or a rare nice thing, an invitation would immediately be given to the neighbors, who would assemble, and they all would have a social time of it. [Thus did they enjoy life with the little they possessed.] There was no distinction in those days in point of dress or grandeur, but all wore their own manufacture.[4] I have heard my grandmother say that when she was dressed in her striped, short, loose gown, and her clean starched and well ironed blue and white checkered linen apron, she felt much better then to appear in a meeting among Christians than she has since when dressed in silks. [The purity of our forefathers taught simplicity of dress, economy in living, morality and contentment as necessary appendages to the Christian religion rather than ostentation and outside show to the neglect of important subjects.] They then had no ruffles, no ribbons, or anything that appeared like ostentation, but all was neat and tidy; as this was the uniform manner of dress in those days, they all enjoyed it without a murmur and felt happy. The men wore garments made of the skins of moose, which they had learned to dress from the Indians; they were, as they said, cold things to put on in the morning, but when once warmed, the cold weather could not penetrate through, and they would last a long time. For shoes, they made of this same kind of skin, a substitute called moccasins, until the country began to be opened a little, and then they got sheep; the wool, the women would card and spin; and such were their habits of industry, as this was a slow way to get their wool worked up, I have heard Grandmother say that she used frequently to work a whole week, both night and day, without undressing herself. She would only lie down for a short time with her clothes on, while carding and spinning; when this was done she would weave it, and then with the bark of some forest tree they would give it a color; without the process of a clothier, or the workmanship of a tailor, they would cut their own garments and make them; and in this cheap, humble, but happy way, these people lived for many years, until the enemy of contentment began to introduce articles of merchandise, which soon created pride, and a sort of rivalship commenced, and as soon as one came in possession of a newly imported dress, it stimulated others to follow the fashion, and one extreme generally follows another. In this way has our country since been infested with this foolish pride of dress, making gay the outside; while some, it is feared, have neglected the most important part, the soul; but another era, it is hoped, will take place, which will yet cause all who watch for it to be more and more happy.

[The inhabitants suffered one great inconvenience for the want of a mill to grind the grain they then raised. Necessity however being the mother of invention, they made for themselves a large mortar to pound their grain with which was simply this, a great log cut six feet in length and set upon one end; the top end they made a hole in, and with a round stick made oval at one end so that it would fit exactly into the mortar, they would pound their grain, which would make it better to cook after being cracked than when whole. In this way they managed until there was a mill built twenty or thirty miles distant. This was quite a journey in the winter as they said the snow would sometimes be six feet deep on an average. At one time Mr. Rosebrook said they could not get there to mill for six weeks, the snow was so deep.]

Now, while living at that time in this country, the greatest disadvantage, which they felt most seriously, was the want of good schools for their children. As they seldom had any schools so near as to have the privilege of sending them at all, their eldest went but one day, their second, one week, which completed their school education. But, as their mother had in early life acquired a knowledge of letters and the proper use of them, she instructed them so well that they could read and spell with considerable accuracy. This they found to be useful in afteryears, as they could read for themselves and sometimes for others. For instance, the husband of the eldest became afflicted with weakness of his eyes, so that he could not himself see to read, and being drawn up with the rheumatism so much that he could not walk, it has been a matter of great consolation to him in his dull hours to sit still and hear her read; and thus time passed more swiftly away than it would have done otherwise.

I have often heard my grandmother tell with great interest the proceedings of former years. One instance, I recollect, was this: that at one time when the state legislature met, a man of rather ordinary appearance presented himself. The members viewed him and then asked him if he was the choice of the people. His answer was this: "Sirs, I am the only man in my town; of course there was no one to set up against me; therefore I considered it my privilege to come here, and I have made my appearance." This caused some glee, but the honest man was not refused a seat. At another time, as the military laws were in those days similar to ours, a neighboring town legally warned a meeting for the purpose of choosing military officers and to have a training. After the officers were chosen there was but one remaining soldier; and he, looking wishfully upon his superiors, said; "Gentlemen, I have one request to make, that is, as I am the only soldier, I hope your honors will not be too severe in drilling me, but will spare me a little as I may be needed another time." He could form a solid column, he said, but it racked him shockingly to display. At another time, when they were to have a training, an officer went fifty miles to Lower Coos, as it was then called, or Haverhill now, for two quarts of spirit, to treat his company with. As they had no carriages in those days, neither had they a road suitable for one, he took his horse, put on the saddle and then a pair of large saddlebags, filled with provisions for the journey, and a jug for the spirit, and provender for his horse; and as they traveled at that time, it took him three or four days to perform this journey. When on his way home, by some unknown accident, the cork got loose, and the bottle was emptied of its contents into the saddlebags. The liquor would have been saved had not the oats soaked up a part of it; he, however, saved enough to treat his company with. They did not require so much then as too many have required since that time.

It had been a matter of considerable inquiry, how they should get a passage through the White Mountains. [As the population began to increase in Coos and also in Essex, Vermont, it was deemed advisable by the people to look out a place where a road could be made so as to reach the easterly part of the state and the coast of Maine.] Two men who went in search, by name Timothy Nash and Benjamin Sawyer, discovered an opening through the Notch. One of them climbed a tree to be sure of the fact. Here one of them lost a mitten, it being on a high hill, and from that circumstance they gave it the name of the Mitten Mountain. When satisfied there might be a way found here to get to the fertile country on the Connecticut river, without going so far round, they gave the information, and were rewarded by having the whole tract of level land given them above the Notch, and it was granted to them by Governor Wentworth in 1773, as Nash and Sawyer's Location, upon condition that they should cut and make a good road through this tract of land, and cause five families to settle on it in five years. This land was surveyed by General Bucknam, a deputy surveyor of public lands then belonging to the Province, now State of New Hampshire. [It was some time after before a regular road was cut out, yet the inhabitants were profited by it as they could perform the journey on foot, which was often done.] They had got some families settled here, and the people had begun to settle in Conway and Bartlett [upon the easterly side of the hills] and likewise in Jefferson [on the westerly side,] all of whom had an example set them by Colonel Whipple from Portsmouth, who for years was a real father to them. He placed them on his land, and all they could raise more than they needed for their families he bought, and paid them honestly to even half a cent. He used to bring from Portsmouth a bag of half cents to make change, for the purpose of being honest himself and trying to make his tenants honest. This little surplus of grain was carefully laid up for the inhabitants in case of their own need, or that of other persons who should move in.

At one time, provisions in Bartlett were scarce, and some of the people took their sacks and money in their hands and came through the woods, a distance of not less than thirty miles, to buy bread. This was refused by the Colonel, saying his own inhabitants wanted all he had; and they were obliged to return empty. They, however, had the precaution to examine and find where the grain was, and shortly afterward returned, and with an auger, bored a hole up through the floor under where the grain was, secured by a lock, held their sacks under, and filled them. When satisfied they stopped the hole with a plug, and then carried the filled sacks on their backs to the woods, where they had handsleighs prepared to draw the grain, and thus returned in safety. The Colonel finding it out, and being sensible of his error, made but little fuss about it, yet took care how he dealt with them afterward.

The inhabitants now while clearing the timber off their lands, made ashes, which were boiled into salts and exchanged for goods. Everything was very dear. As the distance was so great to go round to get to the seaboard, they began to contrive means to go to Portland, or, perhaps, Portsmouth was the first place where they went to market. [The only difficulty which seemed to prevent them from making it a paying business was the transportation.] With one horse fixed to a car, they first went through the woods. The form of the car was simply this: two poles cut ten or fifteen feet in length, the smaller ends serving as thills for the horse to draw by and the larger ends dragging on the ground, and fastened nearly in the middle with some short poles, on which they would place a bag, or other articles of loading. In this way they got along quite well until they came to the Notch. This was a trying place to get through. To go where they now do, was then utterly impossible. They then turned out at the top of the Notch and went over the edge and so managed to get to the top, and by taking a zigzag course, as much as possible, got down; but in doing this there was danger of the horse tipping over, the hill was so steep. And when they returned, they would tie a rope around the horse's neck, to keep him from falling backwards. At one time, however, one horse did so fall; but he was helped up without receiving much injury. At length a committee was chosen to search and look out the best road. They agreed in all places until they came to the Notch. There they held a council. One-half was for making the road on one side of the stream, and the other half, on the other side; but after considerable consultation on the subject, one of them turned and voted to make the road on the side of the Saco, where it is now. Reader, when you pass this place now spoken of, please to look and judge for yourself, if you would devise a way to make a road on the other side of the stream, and then imagine what courage and perseverance our forefathers possessed. They never seemed to take hold of the plow and look back, but drove on.

At this time, Grandfather remained at Guildhall. He had settled on a beautiful piece of land, easy to cultivate, on the Connecticut river, and things began to look flourishing. He seemed to be in a way to live without much hard labor himself, as his two eldest daughters were married, and his four sons growing up to help him. But in this easy situation he could not long remain. Having an ambitious, enterprising, public spirited disposition, and after going to market in the manner spoken of, and knowing there must be more help and perseverance to make this way practicable, he left his situation and volunteered once more to serve the public. In January, 1792, he took his family and moved to Nash and Sawyer's Location, bought out my father, who had some time before bought out three or four settlers who had declined to remain, and had been living there alone, keeping bachelor's hall in one of the small huts they had built.

Soon after this, my father, rather than to be crowded by neighbors, moved twelve miles down the Saco river, where he would have elbow room enough; and then he began in the woods, in what is called Hart's Location, and remains there until this day, making as much improvement as possible, and laboring for the public good; while Grandfather was beginning again in the woods, yea, more than the woods, in the valley of the Amanoosuc, surrounded by mountains on all sides. He afterward sold his farm at Guildhall, and the effects or proceeds he laid out in this lonesome spot, far from any neighbors, twelve miles either way. In a little log cabin they lived many years, suffering all the hardships which might well be expected or borne in this lonely, uncultivated place; and as they were dependent on their neighbors for food, they were obliged to go, or send their children that distance to obtain it, always feeling anxious for their safety when they were gone, fearing some accident might befall them. The way was so rough they were fearful the horse would break his leg and injure the child. Many an hour, I have heard my grandmother say, she has spent in meditation[5] of her absent children; and many times, at a late hour in the night, before they would return; and then she would pour out her love in prayer and thankfulness to her heavenly Father for preserving them, and that she was permitted to receive them again to her humble mansion.

Thus they lived several years, working on their farms and making roads; sometimes for pay and sometimes without pay, just as it happened, until the legislature saw fit to grant them a turnpike in 1803. This was divided into shares to the number of five hundred, and let out to different men to make.[6] After a while, as traveling and business increased, he built a large and convenient two-story dwelling, on an elevated spot, on the west end of what has since been called Giant's Grave, with two rooms underground. From the chamber in the second story was an outside door, which opened so that one could walk out on the hill, which was beautiful, and gave a view of all the flat country around it. He built a large barn, stable, sheds and other out buildings, a saw mill and grist mill, etc.; the latter was of but little use, being one and a half miles from where he lived. The mice injured the bolt so much it was difficult to keep it in repair; but the saw mill was of great service, both to him and to my father, when building.

Thus he prospered and lived well; but his children were not satisfied with their situation; married, and left him, one after another. Their leaving him and setting them off, put him in rather low circumstances in his advanced age; still, he had sufficient, but was in want of someone to help him, as will be shown in the next chapter.

CHAPTER III[1]

——

The Crawfords. Their privations and hardships. Ethan's marriage.

ETHAN ALLEN CRAWFORD was born in Guild-hall, Vermont, in 1792, and when quite young, his parents moved to Hart's Location [Notch of the White Hills,] in New Hampshire, twelve miles from neighbors, one way, and six the other, in a log house in a small opening among the trees. [Preparations were immediately commenced for clearing up for a farm. Young Ethan and his brother, though young, assisted their father in making an opening. They were by nature designed for such an undertaking, being healthy and rugged.]

Here our family lived alone, with the exception of a hired man. One Saturday, my parents went to spend the Sabbath in Bartlett, among the Christians; and they left me and a brother older than I was with this hired man to take care of us, and with a plenty of provisions to last until their return. Soon after they were gone, this man picked up such things as he thought valuable, and what victuals were cooked for us during their absence, started for the woods, and left us, two little boys (to use the words of Ethan), with none to keep us company all night, and without food. We had a cow, but neither of us was large enough to milk her. We, however, got some potatoes, roasted them in the ashes, and ate them; then, being tired and lone-

25

some, we hugged ourselves up together and went to sleep. On Monday, when they came and found us, and things as they were, my father was so incensed with the man for his ill treatment of his little helpless children, that he followed him to Franconia, where he came out of the woods. We recovered some of the stolen articles, and had the man punished for his perfidy.

While my father was clearing up his land, I and my brother helped him all we could. Many times I have chopped, and my hands would swell and pain me in the night so much that my mother would get up and poultice them to give me ease. I never had a hat, a mitten, or a pair of shoes, of my own, that were made for me, until I was nearly thirteen years old. I could harness and unharness horses in the cold winter weather, with my head, hands, and feet nearly bare, and not mind or complain of the cold, as I was used to it; it made me tough and healthy.

After this I was sent to school in the winter, to some one of the neighboring towns, wherever I could work night and morning and help pay my board, until I could read, write, and cipher.

In 1811,[2] I enlisted as a soldier, under the command of Captain Stark, for eighteen months, with a promise from another officer that I should have a commission after we should get to Plattsburgh. Here I staid through the summer; and late in the fall the spotted fever raged in the company, and I was one of the subjects of this contagious disease. I was sick and did not know but that it was even unto death, as numbers were dying daily around me. I was carried to the hospital; but as it was so filled with the sick, I thought I would fare better in my own bunk, and got back there somehow or other. Here I made the best I could of it, and having a strong constitution, as soon as my fever turned, I crawled out and bought me a turkey and had a part of it made into broth, of which I took a little at a time until it strengthened me, and I could get about.

Thinking that if I staid there I would not live long, I made an application for a furlough to go home, which was granted me. I started, but was so weak and emaciated I could walk but a short distance in a day, and when the wind blew I was obliged to stop and lay by, as I could not stand against it. I, however, succeeded in getting home to the White Hills in fourteen days, with the assistance of some kind friends, who would occasionally give me a ride. Once on the way I was suspected of having run away from the army and I was obliged to show my furlough.

In the winter, after regaining my health, I returned to my duty. I afterward had to take the place of a lieutenant, a sergeant, and a corporal, and as I was called upon often-er than many others on duty, one day when I was gone they chose their officers, and I was left out. This dissatis-fied me so much I made my complaints to the man that had promised to raise me above a common soldier. He wrote to Washington, to headquarters, and we soon had an answer saying I might be discharged. This I showed to the officer that had the authority to give the discharge. He was unwilling; but after he had done it, he gave me a corporal's commission, which I accepted, and I stayed for a while. The main army moved off, and I was left with a company of invalids, and not much to do; I thought best to go home, and so I went home.

In 1814,[3] I lived with two men who had engaged to take out the trees by the roots, and prepare for a road sixteen feet wide, leading from Russell, in the state of New York, to St. Johns, for fifty cents a rod. We made a beginning soon after the frost was out of the ground; took our provisions and cooking utensils with us, and there, in those woods, I staid seven months without once coming out. Three men of us, in that time, with one yoke of oxen, grubbed and made a road nearly eight miles long, and then I went home.

In the spring of 1815, as my eldest brother was in Russell, in the state of New York, and I having been there and liking the place, I concluded to go again. I bought a horse and went. The eighth and ninth of June, the ground froze and the snow fell a foot deep or more, and lasted for me to draw logs to a saw mill two days with four oxen.

Here the pigeons were so numerous in some places that the farmers were obliged to watch their fields to keep the birds from picking up the sowed grain. At one time I went with three other men into the woods onto a swell or small ridge of land where the pigeons had made their nests and hatched their young ones, and on half an acre of land, in some beech trees, we found them in great abundance. We would chop one tree and fall it against another, and that would cause the young ones to drop from both trees. Some trees had forty nests in each of them, with two young ones in each nest. These were a clear squad of fat, and as they could only hop along and could not get out of our way, we picked them up and pulled off their heads and took out their crops to keep them from spoiling. There we worked until each of us had as many as we could carry home in a bag on a horse's back; and a greater sight than that I never saw.

Among the numerous branches of business which the man I hired with had for me to do, was working on a river of swift water, where we boated barrels of potash fifteen miles down the river. These barrels weighed five hundred apiece. I could take one of these at a time, of this average weight, and put it into the boat, hoisting it two feet. There was but one other man in the boat that could lift more than one end of a barrel. My strength was so great, and my health so good, I did not know but it would last, until I began to have the rheumatism by being so often and so much exposed, and in the heat of the day and when in a state of perspiration, obliged to go into the water and remain there as we oftentimes had to do.

Here I lived and had bought me a piece of land in the town of Louisville, in the state of New York, and I had made a handsome beginning, intending to settle there near this brother of mine; when, in 1816, we received a letter from our aged grandfather, desiring one of us to come and live with him. He said he would not live long, being troubled with a cancer on his under lip; that his children were all married and settled away from him, such as were capable of taking care of the harvests; and that one of us should have a deed of all his property if he would come and see him, Grandmother, and Uncle William, their eldest son (who was not capable of managing his business through life), and pay his grandfather's honest debts.

My brother, who was always considered the wiser of us two, said he would not do this, and advised me not to; setting forth the many difficulties that would arise on the part of near relatives, who, though not willing to go there themselves, yet might find fault with another's going; and the great responsibility resting upon the one who should undertake the care of old people. Although he honored and respected them, yet he felt inadequate to the task, and thought it devolved upon someone better qualified for it. This counsel I heard and concluded to abide by.

Unfortunately, I got lame and could not work; I therefore thought I would go home and visit them and my parents who lived twelve miles distant from them; and, in December, I started. On my arriving there, the old gentleman expressed marks of gratitude for my obedience to his summons, but as I had made up my mind according to my brother's advice, I told him I had not come to stay, only to see him. On hearing this he put his hand upon my shoulder and entreated me in such a manner, with tears trickling down his furrowed cheeks, that my former resolution was shaken; for he had ever been a kind grandparent to me, and how could I deny him my services now when he so much needed them?

I then concluded to go back to Louisville and sell my possessions there and return to their assistance and do the best I could for them. Accordingly, I went back and sold, and in March, 1817, returned to them again. I brought with me two hundred and eighty dollars which I had earned. This I contributed to the benefit of the farm. Then I gave my notes for a sum of from two to three thousand dollars, and took up his. Afterward he gave me a deed of his farm, by me giving them a mortgage back, for their maintenance through life. I provided every means which he and his friends thought proper to remove the disease, but to no purpose; it was so far advanced it was incurable.

It was now necessary to have a nurse, one who would feel an interest in his being made comfortable, as the disorder so much affected Grandmother she could not dress it, neither could she bear to stay in the room when it was being dressed. And they desired me to go for a cousin of mine, by the name of Lucy, who was a particular favorite of theirs, and get her to come and take care of him. I went and obtained her consent, with that of her parents, who well knew his situation and felt anxious that his last days might be made as comfortable and easy as possible.

The 5th of May, Lucy came home with me and took the whole care of Grandfather; and he was so well pleased with what she did for him that he thought no one else could do for him as well; and would never let his own children dress his lip when she was there. His pains, which were severe, he bore like a Christian, without a murmur or a groan, when awake, and he would frequently say he had no more laid upon him than he was able to bear. He would converse upon death with as much freedom as though he was going to take a long journey into a far country and never expected to return.

He gave Lucy and myself a great many counsels, and expressed a desire, in the course of the summer, that as Lucy took such good care of him, he hoped she would unite with me and continue there to stay; and, in the like manner, rock the cradle for the declining years of Grandmother as she did for him; and likewise for Uncle William, who, he said, might cause some trouble, as most people in his situation possess a quick disposition and would sometimes be irritable. He told us not to mind such things but to discharge a clear conscience toward him, and we should have a reward for it, and if no other, we should have a peace of mind which would surpass everything in this world. He would often say to Lucy when his cancer increased so much as to become an inhabited corruption, that he was only a glass for others to look into and see their own final corruption at death. He would never suffer any one to sit up with him, or even go into his room in the night to ask if he wanted anything; always seeming to be afraid we should do so much for him that we should get sick. In this way he lived from May until September upon nothing but sweetened milk and water, with sometimes a little spirit in it, which he said he could not well do without, as the cancer in his mouth and throat was so offensive to him. When his flesh was all gone, and his teeth fell into his mouth, his spirit left his body without a struggle or a groan, with his hands and eyes uplifted toward heaven; he, by signs, commended Uncle William and Grandmother to my care. [In September, 1817, he departed this life, leaving a large circle of friends and relatives to mourn his loss.] Our good neighbors, who lived at a distance of twelve and twenty miles, assembled and paid their respects to his remains on the 27th.

As Lucy had with so much judgment, alacrity, and perseverance discharged her duty toward Grandfather, and knowing no other that would fill her place, I solicited her to engage with me in the performance of the remaining obligations I was then under. She accordingly agreed to, after I should have obtained the consent of her parents, and on the 1st of November, we were married. She now became a partaker of all my joys and sorrows.

In the winter of 1818, being in good health and possessing a goodly share of strength, I, with the help of Uncle William, managed to do all our own work, without having any other help, as we wished to economize all we could to meet my notes and take them up when they should become due. In this way our honest endeavors were prospered; and I was able to make my first payment without trouble, and after getting through with my spring work, in the summer I hired men and went to labor on the turnpike for pay, laying up everything we could earn and save from our common, necessary living, for that purpose, as I was determined to pay every demand as soon as it should be called for.

CHAPTER IV[1]

———

Burning of the Crawford House.
Sickness of Mrs. Crawford.
Narrow escape from the flames.

EARLY on the morning of the 18th of July, my family
not being well, I went to our nearest neighbors for
some assistance. It was nearly eight o'clock when I returned with Mrs. Rosebrook, and not long after we had a
son born, which weighed nearly five pounds. After doing
what was necessary to be done at the house, at eleven
o'clock I went to carry some dinner to our men who were
at work on the Cherry Mountain road, one and a half miles
from home. Grandmother desired me, on my return, to
bring her some trout, as she said I must give them a good
treat and do something extra for their services and my good
fortune that morning. I accordingly, though reluctantly,
obeyed her commands. The trout were in as great haste for
the hook as I was for them. I caught in a few minutes, a fine
string of good large sized ones. I was gone about one hour
from home, and when on my return, the first sight which
caught my eyes as I came out of the woods, was flames of
fire ascending the tops of the chimneys, ten or fifteen feet
in the air! I added a new speed to my horse, who was then
under a good headway, and I was soon there. Here I found
Lucy and her infant placed on some feather beds behind an
old blacksmith's shop, where she could not see the flames
of fire in the open air. I passed her immediately by and flew

to the house and tried to save something from it, but all in vain, the fire was raging, and to that height I could not save a hive of bees, which stood a few rods from it. These were suffered to perish. There were no men there excepting a Mr. Boardman, from Lancaster, who, with his wife, on their return home from Saco, called for some refreshments, and while this was preparing, Mrs. Boardman came into the room and inquired of Lucy how she did, and what she should say to her mother who lived three miles from them, when she should get home. After a little conversation and receiving thanks from Lucy for her kindness, she took her leave and went out. The room where Lucy lay was about ten feet wider than the other part of the house, which was built with these two rooms underground. And there was a large poplar whose boughs and leaves touched the chamber window where grandmother slept. While in conversation with Mrs. Boardman Lucy saw smoke and leaves pass her window; but as she was much engaged and the wind shifted, she forgot to mention it. The girl, going into one of the rooms, heard the crackling of fire overhead, and when she opened the chamber door, the flames met her. She immediately closed the door and gave information. In a few minutes Mrs. Boardman returned and said, "Mrs. Crawford, do not be frightened, the house is on fire and cannot be saved; be quiet and keep still, you shall be taken care of; remember your life is of more value than all the property which is to be consumed." These words, coming in so friendly a manner, and from so good a woman, calmed all her fears, and, when left alone, she had the presence of mind to command herself without trembling. She arose and dressed herself, then went to the desk which stood in the room, unlocked it, took out all the papers and other things of consequence from the drawers, and put them in a pine chest which stood near by, then asked Mr. Board-man to save it, which he did. She then went into another room and took out some drawers, and they were carried out and saved. She would have taken down the top of a brass clock, had it not been for Mrs. Boardman, who would, every time she saw her making exertions, admonish her by saying she was not aware of her critical situation, and as it hindered her by these arguments from doing much herself, Lucy gave up and was placed in an armchair and carried to the place where I found her. The infant was the last thing taken from the burning ruins, as Mrs. Rosebrook had tak-en it and laid it upon a bench in the barroom, for the house was built for a tavern. Mr. Boardman asked where it was. She said she knew, and ran in and brought it out. We had a pig shut up in a pen so near the building that, before he could make his escape, was burned. The noise of this pig attracted the attention of the other hogs and brought them to the place, and it was with difficulty that Lucy and one little brother of hers, four years old, who lived with us, could keep them from tearing everything to pieces. Beds all on fire—cheeses all around—hogs in the midst of them —all hurly-burly; while the female party had much to do to keep safe what they had taken from the house, and Mr. Boardman had his horse and chaise to look after. As there was but little help, there could not be much saved. The day was fair, and the wind strong, and it blew in different directions, so that the bed on which Lucy lay caught fire three times, which she extinguished by smothering it with her hands.

The fire is supposed to have communicated from a can-dle, accidentally left burning in a kitchen chair, in the morning, in a tightly ceiled room, by our grandmother; and it was some time making its appearance, owing to the

stillness of the air, as that was the place where it was discovered. Lucy having been unwell in the night, the old lady
was called upon to come and see her, and after rendering
her services, Lucy was better and desired her to go to bed
again. This, she was at first unwilling to do; but after a little
persuading, she went. I gave her a new long candle, which
she took and set in the chair, and then she lay down on the
bed, not thinking to sleep, as she said; but she did fall
asleep, and when she awoke, the sun shone brightly in her
face, and thinking she had neglected Lucy, and unmindful
of the candle, left it burning; coming out of the room, she
shut the door after her and came down stairs.

Dear reader, my feelings at this time, may better be imagined than described; no inhabited house within six
miles, on one side, and twelve the other, my family in this
destitute situation, all my carriages sharing the same fate
with the buildings, and no means to convey them hence.
As Mrs. Boardman was a feeble woman, and out of health,
she could not think of giving up her chaise to carry away
my family with; neither was it a desirable carriage for them.
And while we were contriving some means to get them
away, it seemed as though directed by the hand of Providence, a tin peddler happened along, and after we had put
what things we saved into an old barn which stood at such
a distance from the other buildings that it escaped the fire,
he kindly emptied his cart of its contents in the field, and
we placed some feather beds in his cart and put Lucy and
her brother and the babe in it. I then gave the before mentioned trout to Mr. Boardman, helped them to their carriage, and they went their way, and we went ours. While on
the way, the baby was uneasy, and Mrs. Rosebrook picked
raspberries and gave them to the child, and to its mother.
Grandmother and Mrs. Rosebrook on horseback, myself

and the peddler on foot, made up our traveling party, and about the setting of the sun, and over a very rough road, we all arrived in safety at Mrs. Rosebrook's. The two girls we had living with us, staid and slept in the barn, and likewise the men, when they returned from work. I had laid in a good store of provisions for my family's use, as we were not always sure of a crop, and depended on buying. We had a small store pretty well filled with salt and salt fish. I had bought forty dollars worth of wheat and forty of pork. I had made two-thirds of a barrel of maple sugar, and when done sugaring, had taken the large potash kettle which I had used and brought across the Amanoosuc river, I walking over on a log, the kettle on my head, Uncle William helping me to put the kettle on my head; after putting it in a cart I brought it home. These and all other kinds of provisions were destroyed. Some new cheese, however, was saved; this was in the furthermost part of the house, where the fire came last. All my farming tools were destroyed, excepting those that the men had working with, such as plows, harrows, hoes, shovels, rakes, pitchforks, scythes, etc. In the morning we had enough and to spare; in the evening, nothing left but this new cheese and the milk of the cows.

The next day was the Sabbath; the horses were sent for, and the girls came down and joined us. One incident, by the way, I would just relate. The swallows, after losing their nests, followed the family, and the barns of Mr. Rosebrook seemed to be alive with them; they were actually partakers of our trouble.[2]

Monday, my parents and Lucy's came to see what was to be done; and they agreed to move a small house, twenty-four feet square, which belonged to me, one and a half miles from where ours stood before it was burned; and sent an invitation to our neighbors, who immediately collected, with provisions for themselves and oxen, to draw the building.

My loss by the fire was estimated at $3,000, and there was no insurance. I was young and ambitious, but this shock of misfortune almost overcame me; and I was for some days quite indifferent which way the world went. I at length was constrained to arouse my feelings, and once more put my shoulder to the wheel.

My house was placed upon the spot and left, with one outside door, and chimney up as high as the chamber floor; there were no windows, and there was nothing but a rough, loose floor to walk upon. Yet we could not prevail upon Lucy to stay any longer than two weeks where she was. We therefore spread bedclothes for a carpet, and hung some up for a partition, to keep her from taking cold; and, thus situated, she was accidentally visted by several gentlemen and ladies from Portland. They seemed to sympathize with her, and afterward sent her several articles of furniture for the table. Lucy, however, took cold, which caused her some pain and trouble; and she was obliged to go back to Mr. Rosebrook's and remain there three weeks longer.

I hired two joiners and went twelve miles for lumber to work with, and while we were thus engaged, Colonel Binney, from Boston, with two young men, came along, by the way of Littleton, to my place. Finding us so destitute of everything, they staid but a short time and then went down to Father's. The young men wanted to go on the mountain; they consulted him and agreed to take him for a guide, with a man to carry provisions and other necessary things. They rode to the top of the Notch, then sent back their carriage, and proceeded to the woods. They had much difficulty in managing to get through; they, however, proceeded slowly; sometimes crawling under a thicket of trees, sometimes over logs and windfalls, until they arrived where they could walk on the top of trees. This may seem to some strange, but it is nevertheless true. They never reached the summit but managed to get along on some of the hills.

As the day was growing to a close, they returned to the woods, in order to pass the night, and erected a shelter for their protection. A dense fog arose and during the night it rained. In the morning, owing to the darkness, they could not tell the best way to proceed, but took the surest way, by following the Amanoosuc river, and came to my house. These men wore fine and costly garments into the woods, but when they returned, their clothes were torn and much injured by the brush, and their hats looked as if they had been through a beggar's press. They were much exposed all night, without fire or food.

In September, there came two gentlemen to my father's and engaged him to go with them to the top of Mount Washington, where they placed an inscription in Latin, which was engraved on a brass plate, and nailed it on a rock; they likewise filled a bottle and put it in a rock. The inscription was as follows, as I had it copied and kept carefully at home. (I vouch not for the Latin or translation being correct; it is at all events, a true copy, as found on the plate; and was translated, with the exception of the word "*perspire*," by a friend who was afterward in the vicinity.)

"*Altius ibunt, qui ad summa nitunteer.*"—They will go higher who strive to enter heaven. "*Nil reputans, si quid superesset agendum.*"—Think nothing done while anything remains to be done. "*Sic itur ad astra.*"—We go thus to the stars. "*Stinere facto per inhostales sylvas Rustribus pramptis feliciter superrtes. (Eheu quantus adest vius sudor!) Johannes Brazer, Cantabrigsensis, Georgius Dawson, Philadel-*

phiensis, hic posuerant ivid Septembris MDCCCXVIII." —
After passing inhospitable woods, and surmounting abrupt
ledges (how it made us perspire), John Brazer, of Cam-
bridge, and George Dawson, of Philadelphia, placed this
inscription here on the fourth day of the Ides of September, 1818.[3]

We succeeded in having a comfortable, small house, for
the winter 1819. We had now many difficulties to encounter, owing to the limited size of our small house; it being at
that time the principal, if not the only, market road then
traveled by the people who depended upon going to market in the winter with their produce, from the upper part
of New Hampshire, and even west of Vermont; and the
snow did not fall early to make a good sleigh path.[4] When
it did, our house was filled, and Lucy would many times
have to make a large bed on the floor for them to lie down
upon, with their clothes on, and I would build a large fire
in a large rock or stone chimney that would keep them
warm through the night. It was no uncommon thing to
burn in that fire-place a cord of wood in twenty-four hours,
and sometimes more.

At this time my father thought it best to sell, as there
was a chance, he thought; he being holden with me on the
notes, I suppose, would like to have been liberated from
them. He consulted with Grandmother and gave her and
William a mortgage of his farm, at that time worth two of
mine, so that there should be no incumbrance on my barn.
But the man to whom we expected to sell, drew back, and
we still remained and struggled along as well as we could
through the winter.

In the month of May [1819] four gentlemen came on
horseback to visit the mountains. I gave them the best information I could. They set off together and made the best

they could of their excursion through the forests, but suffered considerable inconvenience by the thickness of the
trees and brush, which would every now and then take
hold of their clothes and stop them; [but they succeeded in
reaching the top. After lingering a time, gazing at the hills
and valleys for miles around, they commenced their descent and arrived safely at the house from which they
started,] well satisfied, notwithstanding the unfriendly
brush.

As this was the third party which had visited the mountains since I came here to live, we thought it best to cut a
path through the woods; accordingly my father and I made a
foot path from the Notch out through the woods, and it
was advertised in the newspapers, and we soon began to
have a few visitors.[5] As my accommodations were limited,
small parties were under the necessity of stopping at my
father's, eight miles from the Notch.

This summer I succeeded in removing a barn from the
place where our house had been brought by our neighbors
after the fire, and I converted the barn into a stable for
horses. We considered it quite comfortable for the winter,
and as I had payments to make, I had to work economi-
cally to be able.

I spent the winter of 1820 in doing my own work and assisting the traveler up and down the Notch, and over the
mountains toward Lancaster. As it is a common thing for
the wind to sweep away the snow through the Notch, opening and leaving it bare, so the teamsters required help to
get along, and sometimes they have been obliged to leave a
part of their loads at the Notch House, and I have gone
down there and taken it and conveyed it to the owners, and
on my return would bring home grain and other necessary
things for our use, as I ever calculated to manage so as to

load both ways, and not lose my time or the wear of my horses for nothing.

In March, as I had a famous dog for catching deer, I told Lucy one pleasant morning I was going out to the Notch with my dog, and I hoped to bring a deer home alive and we would tame him. She smiled and said to me she thought I had better give up such an idea as that, for who could catch and halter-break a wild animal like a deer. Never mind, said I, there is nothing like trying. So I took my rope, dog, and snow-shoes, and commenced my journey. After traveling about four miles in the roads, I turned out and went into the woods, say half a mile, when Watch, my dog, gave an alarm, which told me he had found a deer. I went as fast as I could and told Watch to be careful and not hurt the deer. He had found a young buck and stopped him; I went up, and Watch took him by the ear and held him, while I tied on my rope in form of a halter, and then began to descend the hill, and come into the road. He was rather turbulent at first, but soon became quite tame and peaceable, and would smell of my hands, as I perspired some, as if for salt. I brought him home and made a place in the stable and put him in, and Lucy's little brother fed him with cabbage and small pieces of cut potatoes. We kept him until June, when by accident, the little boy happened to leave one whole potato, which got so far into his throat that I could not remove it, and consequently the poor thing died.

In May, there came a gentleman and lady and put up with us for the night; it began to snow, and in the morning the snow was a good twelve inches deep; and they, being in a hurry, were desirous to proceed on their journey but did not know how they could get through the snow with their wagon. I then brought up my horse sled, took off the wheels from their wagon, and placed them and the wagon on the sled, and prepared a seat for each of us to ride comfortably, attached my horse to the sled, and carried them to Bethlehem, twelve miles. As we had now got out of the snowy region, and they could travel by themselves, I assisted in putting their carriage together again, for which he gave me a dollar, and we took our leave of each other, and they pursued their way and I returned home. I went one and a half miles down the Amanoosuc river, or Ompompanusuck, according to the ancient Indian name, and took the frame of an old grist mill, which stood there useless and which belonged to me, and brought it home, having taken it apart, and made a temporary cheese house and had a dairy, and made twelve hundred weight of cheese, which I carried to market in the fall and sold for a good price. This enabled me to make another payment of $200.

This summer there came a considerable large party of distinguished characters, such as the author of the New Hampshire map, etc., to my house, about noon, to ascend the mountains and give names to such hills as were unnamed, and after a dinner of trout, they set out, taking me for a guide and baggage-carrier.

[Editor's note: In Lucy Crawford's manuscript the names of the "distinguished characters" are given; they will be found in this edition in Chapter I, page 9. In the edition of 1846 the passage describing the naming of the peaks directly follows the passage above, in the same paragraph. I have transposed this passage to Chapter I where it will be found on pages 9-10.]

In September, at one time, there came a number of gentlemen up through the Notch, and sent [word] to me [that they wished to see the top of Mount Washington and requested ⟨me⟩] to prepare and furnish them with provisions and other necessaries for the expedition. I was accordingly fitted out, and when ready, my pack weighed eighty pounds. I carried it to the Notch on horseback, and when I arrived there the sun was setting, and the party had taken the path and gone along and left their cloaks by the way for me. I piled them on top of my load and budged on as fast as possible, and when I arrived at the camp it was dusk; there was no fire; wood was to be chopped, and supper to prepare, and when all this was done, I was tired enough to sleep without being rocked in a cradle.

In November I went on the hill in front of my house, south, and there set up a short line of sable traps, twenty-three in number, and caught twenty-five sables of fine quality and one black cat, or fisher.[6]

The winter of 1821 I spent doing my own work and buying salt, and transporting it from Portland to Lancaster, and exchanging it with the merchants for grain and other things for my family's use. And as I had been somewhat unlucky with my pet deer last summer, I thought to try again for another, and in a manner like the former one, I prepared and went near the same place. I found several, one of which I took alive. This was a beautiful young doe and she was with young. I now felt quite rich in taking this prize. I suppose my feelings were similar to those spoken of by Robinson Crusoe, when he succeeded in taking the llamas on the island. I did not know but that they might increase; we could build a park and keep them, as these animals are easily tamed, and then I should have them to show our visitors in the summer when they came. Perhaps I could now and then spare one for the table, if requested by them; but alas! this was only imaginary, like the fable of the maid and her milk pail. I put on my rope in the same manner as I did the former one, and began to try to lead

her, but I could do nothing with her; she would not walk
with me, so I shouldered her and brought her into the road;
this made quite a load for me to travel with, as I was then
four miles from home; but said I to myself, without some
pain there will be no gain; so I made the best I could of it,
and when in the road would often set her down and try to
lead her, but I could not. This was not exactly like the one
I had taken the preceding year, it was of a dark brown color.
After I got her home, I had either hurt her in bringing her
home, or she was so delicate she would not partake of food,
and to put her out of misery, I concluded we had better
dress her. This was as fine a piece of venison as I had ever
seen. Now as I had not saved this one's life, I said I would
go again; so I went, and my dog started a good sized buck
and followed him toward home, and near the road he had
stopped him and then waited for me to come up and take
him, and while there they were observed by some travelers
passing along at this time, before I had time to come up
with him, although I made long strides on my snow-shoes,
as I feared something would happen to him. When I came
up, I found the traveler had been to the house and obtained
a gun and shot him, and to my great mortification I found
him dead, with the man exulting in triumph over this great
feat which he had performed. I then told him the great disappointment which he had unconsciously given me; but as
he was dead, it was of no use to make many words about it,
so he helped me to bring him home, and here he was served
like the former one, and sent to Portland.

In March, I hired Esquire Stuart to come with his compass and go into the woods and see if there could not be a
better and more practicable way found to ascend the mountains. We set out with provisions, blankets, fireworks, and
snow-shoes for the woods. We set our compass, and spotted

trees, which made a line to be followed at another time. When night came on, I built a camp and struck up a fire. We ate our supper and retired with our dog quietly to rest. We spent three days in making this search, and returned well satisfied we had found the best way; for the road which we had heretofore traveled was an uneven one, going up a hill and then down again, and this in so many successions, that it made it tiresome to those who were not accustomed to this kind of journeying. The way[7] which we had now found was over a comparatively level surface for nearly seven miles, following the source of the Amanoosuc, or Ompompanusuck, until we arrived at the foot of Mount Washington, and then taking a ridge or spur of the hill. We could now ascend without much difficulty, and found there might be a road made, with some expense, sufficiently good so that we might ride this seven miles, which we thought would facilitate the visitor very much in his progress; and, to add to my encouragement, some gentlemen from Boston made a subscription in 1823 to this purport: that, providing I should make a good carriage road, and have it passable in three years, they would be holden to pay the sums which were set against their respective names; and we had nearly $200 subscribed for this purpose; but as I was already under so much embarrassment I did not feel able to build an addition to my house, and I well knew that if I made this road, and did not have suitable accommodations for those who would be likely to come, it would only be imposing upon the public to have a road to the mountain and not have house room enough to make those comfortable who came to stay with us. I, therefore, was obliged to give up this generous offer of theirs, and at my own expense do what I could from one year to another; but still intending to do everything in my power to make all happy as possible in my humble situation.

In the summer, just before haying, I hired men and went with them to cut this path, and while in the woods, at the distance of three miles from home, as I was standing on an old log chopping, with my axe raised, the log broke, and I came down with such force that the axe struck my right ankle and glanced, nearly cutting my heel cord off; I bled freely, and so much so that I was unable to stand or go. The men that were with me, one a brother of mine, and another stout man, took the cloths we had our dinner wrapped in, and tied up my wound as well as they could, and then began to contrive means to get me out of the woods. [Three miles in the forest and no road rendered it impossible to get a horse.] They cut a round pole, and with their frocks which they wore tied me in underneath it, and thought they could carry me in like manner as we bring dead bears through the woods; but in this way I could not ride. They then let me down and took turns in carrying me on their backs until we got out of the woods; and then one of them came home and got a horse, upon whose back I was helped; and I thus rode home with both feet on one side in ladies' fashion, and when I arrived there I was assisted in alighting. There happened to be at my house then, a Mrs. Stalbard, who is known in our country and bore the name of Granny Stalbard, whose head was whitened with more than eighty years; who ought to be remembered for the good she had done, and many sufferings and hardships she endured to assist others in distress, and who seemed to be raised for the same end for which she lived in those days. She was an old Doctress woman; one of the first female settlers in Jefferson, and she had learned from the Indians the virtues of roots and herbs, and the various ways in which they could be made useful. Now the old lady said it was best to examine this wound and have it properly dressed; but as it had stopped bleeding I told her I thought it better to let it remain as it then was; but she thinking she was the elder, and knew better, unwrapped it, and it soon set bleeding afresh, and it was with difficulty she now stopped it.[8] She, however, went into the field, plucked some young clover leaves, pounded them in a mortar, and placed them on my wound; this stopped the blood so suddenly that it caused me to faint; this was a new thing to me—a large stout man to faint!—which made me feel rather queerly, but there was no help for it. This wound laid me up pretty much the rest of the summer, but still we persevered, and these men, with some others, finished cutting the path through the woods. So it is that men suffer various ways in advancing civilization, and through God, mankind are indebted to the labors of men in many different spheres of life.

Visitors to the Mountains. Anecdotes of
Ethan A. Crawford.
Mount Deception.

EVERY season brought more visitors to the mountains than the preceding one. Early] this fall Captain Partridge, [who was at that time keeping a military school at Norwich, Vermont,] came with a number of cadets to ascend the mountain, and as I was not able to walk, we were under the necessity of sending for our nearest neighbor, Mr. Rosebrook, to guide them; and likewise at other times, we were obliged to send for him to guide gentlemen up the hills.

At this time, there was to be a general muster at Lancaster, and as I was lame and not able to walk, Lucy was anxious to visit her parents in Guildhall, just opposite that place, and we concluded to go and see them; and on the day appointed, I, with others, went to see the soldiers perform; [upon such occasions there were always a few to be found upon the field who were not so well filled with the spirit of '76 as they were with the spirit of the bottle;] and while I was sitting down on the ground, there came a man who was celebrated for wrestling, and laid hold of me and stumped me to throw him. I eased him off, and then he went to others in the same way, and received similar treatment, until he upset a whole row of old men sitting on a rail fence or board. He came again and insisted upon my

taking hold with him. I told him I was not in the habit of
that kind of sport, and also, I was lame and could not if I
had a disposition to; and he came the third time and
caught hold of my vest and rent it several inches in length,
and at the same time with his foot gave me such a blow on
my lame ankle that the hurt raised my temper to such a
degree that, unconscious of what I did, I put my fist in
such an attitude that it laid him prostrate on the ground.
He was taken up with rather a disfigured face; for which I
was immediately sorry, for I knew he was influenced by
liquor; but it was done, and many were glad of it, while I
was ashamed to think I had given way to passion, and
when I came to where Lucy was, I asked her to forgive my
imprudence by mending my vest. I told her it should be
the last time I would give way to an angry passion, and I
have thus far kept my word.

On August 31, 1821, there came three young ladies, the
Misses Austin, who were formerly from Portsmouth, to
ascend the hills, as they were ambitious and wanted to
have the honor of being the first females who placed their
feet on this high and now celebrated place, Mount Washington. They were accompanied by their brother and
Charles J. Stewart, Esq., who was then engaged to one of
them, and married her, July 4, 1822, and Mr. Faulkner,
who was then a tenant on their farm in Jefferson, attending with their baggage. They were provided with everything necessary for the expedition, and set forward. They
went as far as the first camp that night, dividing it into two
apartments, and then put up. The next morning they
pursued their way until they reached the next camp,
which they in like manner divided. It came on unfavorable weather, and now being in pretty good quarters, they
staid and waited for a better prospect. And as their store
of provisions began to fall short, Mr. Faulkner came in and

said that I must, if I possibly could, go and relieve him, as he had grain out in the field, then suffering, and they wished to have me accompany them.

I now mustered all my courage, as I was then lame, took a load on my back and a cane in my hand to help my lame foot, which was now healed over, and went and overtook them. The weather also looking favorable, we ascended at six o'clock in the morning, and reached the summit just as the sun had got to the meridian. What a beautiful sight! We could look over the whole creation with wonder and surprise, as far as the eye could extend, in every direction, and view the wonderful works of God! Every large pond and sheet of water was plain to be seen within the circuit of one hundred miles for some time, until the sun had got up so high as to cause a vapor to rise from the waters; this, also, was grand to see; the commencement of the little vapor, which would grow larger and larger, until it made a cloud and entrenched the view. Houses and farms were to be seen at a distance, so far off that they appeared nothing more than small specks. [Villages and farm houses appeared like vessels upon the broad ocean.] At one time previous, when here with some gentlemen, we counted forty-two different ponds in different directions. The Sebago Pond is distinctly to be seen, and some have thought they could see the ocean from this place; but as there is no object beyond, it appears to look like a cloud, differing only a trifle in color from the sky. The ladies returned,[2] richly paid for their trouble, after being out five days and three nights. I think this act of heroism ought to confer an honor on them, as everything was done with so much prudence and modesty by them; there was not left a trace or even a chance for a reproach or slander excepting by those who thought themselves outdone by these young ladies.

The winter of 1822, as my ankle was weak, and the rheumatism now found its way to it, I staid at home as much as possible, doing only what necessity really compelled me to, and in the spring I made a considerable improvement on my mountain road. That summer I went on the mountain with one gentleman, and as he was a good traveler, we reached the top of the mountain and returned to the camp before sunset. He proposed coming home that night, so we took some refreshments and started and came along until it grew quite dark, and I proposed to take a little nap and wait for the moon to rise and give us some light. He hesitated a little in consequence of the wild beasts, which he said might happen along and take us while sleeping. I advised him to calm his fears for my faithful dog would keep watch.[3] We took our blankets and lay down and soon fell asleep. Presently there came a large bear spattering along in full speed, and as the air came along with him he did not perceive us until within a few feet of us, and then the dog sprang up and went after him; this awakened us, and as the moon had now got up so high as to shine among the trees, we could pursue our path quite well, and arrived home about twelve o'clock.

We set traps, and caught two at one time, and some more at other times this season, from which we obtained considerable oil.

In August we had some young gentlemen from a university. They were preparing for the ministry, and as they needed exercise and a respite from their studies, they chose this place to spend their leisure hours and regain their strength, and view and contemplate upon the works of God, and climb the mountain. I went with them as guide, and on the way I tried to shorten the distance and make their toil less tiresome by some anecdotes and telling some little stories; but as this did not coincide with their feelings, I gave up these trifles, and remained silent most of the way; and when arriving at the summit, they on this high and elevated spot offered prayers to Almighty God for his goodness. This was, I think, the first prayer I ever heard on this mountain. This appeared solemn—now so high in the air, where we could look down upon inferior objects—what could be more interesting?

The same month others came, and among them was a sea-captain, a man of good stature and heavy; he, while coming down from the hill, and in the act of jumping from one stone to another lying there promiscuously, slipped and unfortunately sprained his ankle. This was some trouble to him the rest of the way; however, he managed to get home. This was the greatest injury happening to any person while going up or coming down the hills, to my knowledge, during our stay at the White Mountains.

This summer we had some trouble with Uncle William, as brother had predicted when he told me if I should go up there I must expect trouble from near relatives. As our situation was so uncomfortable, Grandmother was under the necessity of making my father's house her home, and she was desirous of having William live with her; yet she did not complain of his being ill treated, but wanted him, and coaxed him to go there and live with her. But he did not stay long, as they could do without him. They advised him to come home again, but this was contrary to the old lady's feelings, and she then advised him to go and live with his brother, and as he had ever been at her command, he obeyed her and went. But this was not home to him; and after a while he returned and said he would not be controlled any more but would remain on his farm; he therefore came back and received from us as good treatment as he ever had done.

In September, as I was ascending the mountain with two young gentlemen, we saw in the path, at some distance from the camp, a large bear's track, but saw nothing of the bear. On our descent, near this place, the dog left us, and in a few minutes went to barking in great earnest. I said he has something. I went a few steps and saw a cub, the bigness of a good-sized cur dog, climbing a tree. How we could get him was the next thing. We talked it over and agreed that one should stand in the road and keep watch for the old one, whom we expected should she hear the cries of her cub, and the other should climb the tree and get him off, while I and the dog should remain at the foot of the tree and take him. The cub was followed up the tree in good style. He then walked out on a limb, and from that into a small tree, which I took hold of and shook so hard that he fell off, and the dog caught him. I then took hold of him, and tying his mouth with my handkerchief, brought him safely home and kept him some time. At length a hired man set up a pole and tied a leather strap around his neck and gave him a trough of water to bathe in. This he enjoyed remarkably well for a while, but when the strap stretched he slipped out his head and said, I suppose, good day.

This winter, 1822, I spent in buying salt and transporting it from Portland to Colebrook and exchanging it for grain; I likewise bought a nice mare, for which I paid in salt. I transported the salt with this mare by sleigh loads. This winter my dog caught a great many deer, and would go with anyone who desired him; but an enemy wanted him, and as he could not have him, because he was engaged, he gave him poison; and I lost my famous dog. But shortly after, I bought another equally as good.

In June, when returning from the camp in company with two young gentlemen, as we were traveling along we

Willey House before slide

Willey House after slide

Two camps before slide

Two camps after slide

saw a bunch of mountain ash; they stopped, and each cut for himself a beautiful, nice, and straight cane, which they intended to carry home with them; and after this was done, we again pursued our path, I forward, and they after me, in Indian file, as this was the manner in which we used to travel. The one behind saw another bunch from which he thought he could select a better cane. He stopped to cut it, while we were walking on; and he, being in a hurry, after he had cut this, to overtake us, unmindfully crossed the path and steered directly into the woods. The other one that was next to me, observing his companion was not with us, was alarmed, saying he was subject to fainting fits, and thought he must have fainted. I immediately threw off my load and ran back to where I supposed we left him; there I holloed as loud as my lungs would admit a number of times. He at length heard, and stopped. He was completely lost and could not find his way back. He answered, and I went to him and put him in the right path again. This frightened me more than all the bears in the woods; but it however served as a lesson to others, never to give up a certainty for an uncertainty.

The summer of 1823, Chancellor Kent[4] from New York, came to my house with two young gentlemen. As he was desirous of passing this way, he hired a private conveyance here after leaving the stage, which did not then pass through the Notch as the mail was then sometimes transported on horseback and sometimes in a one horse wagon. He chartered me to carry them to Conway, when they would take the stage again. After putting up with our accommodations through the night, in the morning I harnessed my two mares, who had each a young colt, and they took the road forward and their mothers behind, which made a regular team; this amused them much. I carried them to the destined place the same day; and while on the way, we had an interesting time in exchanging jokes, etc.

In July, another man and myself took blankets, provisions, and other necessary things for a small party who were going to stay the second night on Mount Washington, as they were desirous of being there and seeing the appearance of the sun when it should set in the evening and rise in the morning. After staying at the foot of the hill over night, we ascended, and being there in season, went to work and built three stone cabins. We then collected a quantity of dry moss, laid it in them for beds, spread our blankets, and at an early hour, on this elevated spot, retired to rest, now prostrate on the ground so much nearer Heaven than what we had ever been accustomed. Our sleep was not exactly sound, but was interrupted by dreams, which one would naturally suppose would be the case. In the morning we awoke betimes to view the object we came for. We had the advantage of our neighbors in seeing the appearance of light first; and when the sun rose, it came up, as it were, behind a veil, and appeared the bigness of a good sized cart-wheel. We could look upon it without straining our eyes, as well as we can look upon the full moon; and then it rose from behind this cloud, and came out in its full splendor and glory. This was the first night I ever slept on Mount Washington. One of the party made the following lines:

> The Muses' most inspiring draught,
> From Helicon's pure fountain quaff'd,
> What is it, to the rising sun,
> Seen from the top of Washington!
>
> Canst thou bear a dreary night?
> Stranger! go enjoy the sight.

We then returned over Munroe, Franklin, and Pleasant mountains, following our old path, came in at the Notch, and from there home.

It was now beginning to be fashionable for ladies, attended by gentlemen, to visit this place, both for health and amusement, and we were most of the time crowded. As our house was so small, we could accommodate but a few at a time, although we could give them clean beds; but they were obliged to stow closely at night, and near the roof, as we had but two small sleeping rooms down stairs, and these were generally occupied by ladies; the gentlemen were under the necessity of going upstairs, and there lay so near each other, that their beds nearly touched; but as we did all we could for them, they seemed satisfied with it.

In August, there came at one time three different parties, which made quite a number for us in those days. Early in the morning, the gentlemen set out for the hills, leaving the ladies to amuse themselves and achieve such victories as they, in their capacity, might think proper. After dinner, the ladies inquired if the hill north of my house had ever been visited and whether there were any views that were interesting? And after receiving an answer in the affirmative, they started and took the nearest route, which was a very rough one. One of them being active and ambitious, said she would be the first one up. She then set out in great haste, supposing that this could be done in a few minutes. The day being warm, she soon grew fatigued, and perspiring freely, she gave out before she had attained half its summit, and returned nearly exhausted. She said this hill should bear the name of Mount Deception, for its deceptive appearance; and, from this circumstance, it has since been called by that name. The other ladies, taking it with more moderation, reached the top of the hill; here they could see some habitations in Bethel, and had a good prospect of the valley and the way in which we travel to go up the mountain, which is a delightful view. They returned in a different way. In the evening I amused them with the sound of my long tin horn, sent me by a gentleman from Portland for the benefit of the echo, which, when the horn was sounded, would vibrate along the side of the hill until the sound would die away on the ear. This had a strange effect on one lady, as she said it seemed when the horn was sounded as if it were answered by a supernatural voice from Heaven, inspiring her with strange ideas or feelings, which she never before experienced.[5]

Again, we had another party come, from which I will relate a circumstance. We went up the mountain, the weather then looking favorable, until we reached the top of the hill, and then we went into a cloud, which was dark all around us. Having reached the summit, and not having any landmarks to direct us back, and not being acquainted with the weather here, we staid only long enough for them to carve their names, and then tried to return; but I was lost, myself, for a short time. I started toward the east, and we wandered about until we came near the edge of a great gulf. Here we staid and amused ourselves by rolling such large stones as we could find loose, and these being started, went with such force that they would take others with them, and then rest only in the valley beneath. Although a little danger was encountered in this kind of sport, had one of us slipped accidentally and been precipitated down the gulf, yet it was actually a grand sight; and while we were enjoying this, there came up a strong wind and carried away the clouds in as short time as they had been gathering and coming on. Now what a contrast, to have the darkness all taken away, and then a perfect, clear sunshine come on. It cheered all hearts. We then had a good prospect of all the country around, and this opportunity was not lost. We could see what course to steer, beat our way toward the path, and succeeded in finding it, and returned home.[6]

CHAPTER VI

——

Mountain showers. Trapping the gray cat,
or Siberia lynx. Winds in the Notch.

THUNDER showers about the mountains often arise almost without a minute's warning to those trying to gain the summit. Mr. Crawford relates an account:]

At another time I went up the mountains with two gentlemen. We started in the morning with the prospect of a clear day, and having attained the summit, could see the clouds gathering below us; and as the lightning streaked along in the clouds, a rumbling noise was heard, but not like the sound of thunder. Here, as there was nothing to give it an echo, it only sounded like a rumbling noise in the distance, but it was near us. What a situation to be placed in so high in the air! Like the eagle, we could now look down upon a raging storm, while the atmosphere above was perfectly clear. We then went down to Blue Pond, and, while here, the wind came up, attended with hail, which descended with such violence that it seemed as though every hail stone left a mark on our faces; and to prevent losing our hats, we were obliged to tie them on with our handkerchiefs.[1] We went struggling against the wind a distance of one and a half miles; sometimes it was with difficulty we could stand or walk until after we had attained this distance; we then got below the wind, and could now pursue our way home in a moderate rain. We arrived there completely drenched.

Two gentlemen from Boston came and went up the mountain. After remaining on its summit as long as they wished, returned by the way of Blue Pond, and from thence down Escape Glen, as they termed it, to the camp —a passage romantic, but precipitous, where one of them, as they said, came near losing his life by taking hold of an old root of a tree to support himself which gave way. He was over a perpendicular precipice of fifty feet, but fortunately saved himself and returned safely home. He experienced no injury, save that of being frightened.

This spring and summer, [of 1823,] the gray cat, or Siberia lynx, troubled us very much, making several depredations among our sheep and geese, and we underwent some fears for the safety of our children [when sent any great distance to school or on an errand.] These cats were bold and not afraid of man, never putting themselves much out of the way to shun him. At one time a gentleman was coming down Cherry Mountain in a sleigh, and saw two of these animals engaged in a quarrel, as it appeared to him, in the road before him; and it was with some difficulty that he could convince them that the road belonged to him; but with some entreaties, they separated, one on either side, giving him just room to pass. He said he might have reached them with his whip, but as they were content to let him pass, he was content not to disturb them in their angry looking position. I set traps and in various ways tried to catch them. I even killed a hen and set her for bait, feathers and all on, in the appearance of life, supposing they would like this, but they only seemed to amuse themselves by this in coming up and looking at it and then passing on. At length I thought of one more thing to try. I took some pickled fish, which had a strong smell to it, for bait; and the first one afterward who happened this way, had the curiosity to see what was there; and as the trap was between him and the fish, he put his foot in the trap and was held fast. He managed to move the trap a little distance, but was soon fastened by the grapple, which caught in a thicket, where I found him. He was lying partly hid, and I did not perceive him until I came near stepping upon him, when he suddenly started up, and I as soon sprang back to find something to defend myself with; and when prepared, entered into an engagement with him, which was rather a tough one, he having the advantage, being in the thicket. I conquered him at last and brought him home in triumph; he measured six feet and over. In this, and similar ways, I caught six of them. The next spring I took one by stratagem as I was traveling down through the Notch with a team and dog. Below the Notch House, while we were going on, my dog came upon the track of one of these animals who had just crossed the road before us; the dog followed so closely that the animal sprang into a tree, and then the dog sat at the bottom, barking earnestly at him. I knew he had something, and leaving my team in the road, took my small axe with me, which I always carried, and went to him; he was up a tree thirty feet, watching the movements of the dog. I then cut two birch sticks, the longest I could select, and twisting the ends put them together, and at one extremity of the stick I made a ring with a slip noose to it; this I ran up through the boughs of the tree, and so managed to get it over his head, then giving a sudden jerk, brought him down ten feet; he caught on a limb, and the halter slipped off. I then fixed it again, and he being nearer, gave me a better chance. I put it over his head, down on his neck, so that it held him fast, and then giving another jerk, fetched him to the ground. The dog instantly seized him, but the cat soon extricated himself by tearing him with his claws, which he seemed to know how to apply very actively, causing the dog to cry for quarter. The cat then gave a jump the length of the stick, over a spruce top four feet high, with the halter still around his neck, and here he hung; I then fell to beating him with a club, which I had previously prepared, and the dog, recovering himself, assisted me, and we soon finished him. Shouldering my booty, I returned to my team, and placing him on it, carried him down to my father's, and there leaving him, resumed my journey. On my return I took him home. I never saw but one afterward, and that as I was coming down Cherry Mountain; the dog drove him into a tree, and I followed him up there, myself; but the trees were so thick that he jumped from one to another, and thus made his escape, for the time. But shortly after, I had a trap set in a brook, near the mouth, where it empties into the Amanoosuc, hoping that I might catch an otter; the trap set near the end of a log which crossed the stream, and was fastened by a chain to a limb, six feet above the water, and this cat, wanting to cross the brook here, walked on the log, when, stepping off, he put his foot in the trap, and there he was held. He managed to get back on the log, and then on the limb, and wound up the chain in such a manner, that he could not get either way; here I found him, dead, suspended between heaven and earth. On these animals I had a premium of three dollars apiece, which nearly paid me for my loss and trouble. After making this havoc among them, I was never troubled with any of them again while living at the Hills, and there being no signs of them, I supposed I destroyed the whole family.[2]

In October[3] there came to my house a family from Portsmouth who had hired a man to carry them to Jefferson in a coach, and it had begun to snow before they arrived here, and they concluded to put up with me for the night, and had it not been for this circumstance, they would have had time to have finished their journey that night. The next morning, as it continued to snow, the man hired me to carry them the rest of the way, and the other returned home. They staid the next day, and the second morning, as it had done snowing, I harnessed up two horses and put them on before a good yoke of oxen and commenced my task; and when going over Cherry Mountain, the snow was plumb two feet deep. We worked hard all day to get twelve miles; there I staid over night, and the next day I made out to get home again. This snow all went off before winter.

I had this fall engaged the Notch House[4] and agreed to furnish it with such things as are necessary for the comfort of travelers and their horses. It is the case sometimes in the winter that if no one lived here, people, it seems, must suffer with the cold, for the wind comes down through the narrows of the Notch with such violence that it requires two men to hold one man's hair on, as I have heard them say. I have never found it to blow so hard here as to equal this, yet it has blown so hard as to take loaded sleighs and carry them several rods to a stone wall, which was frozen down so firmly that it was impenetrable, and there the sleigh stopped. I heard a second-hand story from a clergyman that the wind was once known to blow so hard here that it took a log chain and carried it to the distance of a mile or more; but I do not tell this as a fact, only as a story which is told, and perhaps believed by some credulous folks who live at a distance and form strange ideas of this place. At one time I was going down to the Notch House with a load of hay, to an occupant there, when going round the elbow of the Notch there came a gust of wind and upset my load toward the gulf; I instantly turned myself and placed my feet against the railing on the road that was put there for the purpose of keeping horses from running off, which, if I had not done, my load must have gone over a precipice of a hundred feet, with the horses attached to it, and I cannot say where I should have been.[5]

Here I waited until the wind abated, and then I put my shoulder under and righted it again and went on. At another time some young people were going down here, and at or near the top of a long hill, one of the company's horses made a misstep and fell. In the fall, by some means or other, the horse entirely cleared himself of all his harness and lay by the side of the road, while they were permitted to pass by and go a considerable distance by themselves, and the horse stopped yet behind, which made sport enough for the rest of the company for some time.

The winter of 1824 I bought hay at Jefferson, and carried it sixteen miles to furnish the Notch place with; and I had been advised by my friends to build an addition to my house, which I was at first rather unwilling to do, owing to my limited circumstances, not yet being extricated from my first obligations; however, I commenced drawing lumber from Bethlehem, a distance of twelve miles, and this work, with drawing hay and other necessary business, occupied my whole time for this winter. In the spring I hired hands and went industriously to work and soon had a frame thirty-six by forty feet, two stories high, and it was raised by thirteen hands. This was thought to be sufficiently large to accommodate all who would be likely to call upon us. During the summer and fall we had the outside finished and painted. In July, we had a number of excellent gentlemen, some of whom were from the Southern states, to visit us, who gave us an account of their manner of living there, and a description of the country, manners, etc., which was interesting; and another gentleman, a painter, from a different part of the country, who took some beautiful sketches of the hills and likewise of the Notch, which sketches, I presume, have been finished and presented to the public.

In August, we had another party who ascended the mountain, and while there the clouds passed swiftly from under us and a rumbling noise of thunder was heard, which excited a clergyman, one of the party, who offered up a very appropriate prayer to Almighty God, and then we sung "Old Hundred" in the lines set to that tune.

CHAPTER VII

———

Mr. Crawford provides a tent for "Tip-Top."
National convention on "Tip-Top."
Extracts from the Crawford House album.

THIS summer,[1] owing to the dampness of the place on Mount Washington where we built stone cabins, [it was not considered healthy to remain over night;] we never but once afterward slept in them. I went to Portland and there bought a marquee, for which I paid twenty-two dollars, sufficiently large for eighteen persons to sleep under at a time; and a sheet iron stove, for which I paid six dollars; and these I carried on or near the top, spreading our tent near a spring of water which lives here. Our tent, with the tackling belonging to it, I had put up in as small a compass as possible, and it weighed eighty pounds and over. I then took it on my back and carried it almost the whole distance myself; but I had some visitors then going up with me, and one who looked and thought he felt as stout as I was, kindly offering to assist and relieve me, took my load, but could not carry it far before he was satisfied with it. He then laid it down and I took it again and conveyed it the remainder of the way; and on the way we cut a pole to stretch this round, and I carried that up also.[2] This, however, did not last long, as the storms and wind are so violent here that we could not keep it in its place, and it soon wore out. At the same time we carried up a piece of sheet lead which I had purchased, eight or ten feet in length, seven inches wide, and the thickness of pasteboard; this was put round a roller, which I made for the purpose, for the benefit of those who went up and wished to leave their names, which they could now do much quicker and easier with an iron pencil which I made, than they could carve them with a chisel and hammer on a rock. [The violence of the wind and storms soon rent the tent, and to Ethan it proved but a poor speculation. It is with difficulty at the present day with the aid of stone and mortar for a person to be secure from water within the walls of the "Tip-Top" houses.]

Shortly after this, a gentleman from Boston came and went up the hill without a guide, and while on the summit of this majestic mountain, he thought it a favorable occasion to reconsider the doings of the meeting held at the same place on the 27th day of July last by Thomas C. Upham and others. He called a meeting for the purpose, and as no other prominent personage seemed to offer, he was invited to take the chair, *nemine contradicte.* He fully explained the object of the meeting, to wit: to select a suitable man to govern this mighty people. He soon heard the name of the Hon. Jas. Kent, late Chancellor of New York, called out from all parts of this immense canopy, under which our meeting was held. On taking the vote, it was unanimously agreed to recommend him as a candidate to fill the highest office in this republic. When he declared this vote, applause, long and loud, rent the sky, the echo of which still fills his ears. Believing the above nomination will be hailed with joy by those who wish a *virtuous man,* unused to intrigue, to rule over us, and who are *heart-sick* of cabal, political juggling, and roguery, he hereby published it to the nation, believing it his duty so to do. He then returned home well satisfied with the pro-

ceedings of the day; an account of which he published in
the album [belonging to the house] and left. I have here
transcribed it, to show how many different objects are
sought on these mountains.

September 10, another party ascended the mountain;
the day was clear and warm; they found ice in great
quantities, from four to six inches thick.

October 2, Captain Partridge came with fifty-two cadets,
and as I was gone from home, Lucy managed and got
along with them as well as she could. It was not far from
the middle of the day when they arrived, and the Captain,
as he had been there before, took a part of them and
proceeded toward the camp that night for the purpose of
having the next day before him to make some barometrical
observations, and the others went the same afternoon
down to view the Notch and its wonders. Thence they
returned the same evening and staid with us that night.
Lucy gave them all the beds she then had, which was not
enough to accommodate them. Some slept on the floor,
and some slept in the barn, and at one time a number
stacked themselves up in a pile by the side of the fence, in
the bright moonshine; but this was not a very comfortable
situation, for the bottom ones removed their quarters and
returned to the barn. The next morning after breakfast,
they took a guide and went and met the Captain and his
party coming down the hill; they, however, went up, and
back as far as the camp, and there staid that night, while
the former party came home, and the next morning they
all came together again to breakfast. We had one room
half the bigness of the house, which we used as a kitchen,
a victualing room, a sitting room, and when crowded, a
sleeping room; but we were a little better off at this time,
having a cooking stove in a woodshed adjoining the house,

but this place was not large enough to do all the work in, therefore we had to use the kitchen to do the rest of the work in. Though suffering all these inconveniences, Lucy never murmured or complained, but bore them with patience, saying there was an overruling Providence in all these things, and that these and some other difficulties were to try us, and she would always put some good construction on everything, and view things on the bright side, and in this way we got along and lived peaceably together without any difficulty.

In the winter of 1825, I bought brick for a chimney, and had to draw them twenty-one miles, which made quite a job of it; the lumber I had to draw from twelve to twenty miles. This, with what other work I had to do, made a good winter's work for me. The doors we had made in the winter, and in the spring the joiner came and finished his work; and then the mason and painter completed the rest, so that we had a house for our summer company, which increased yearly.

At this time we began to feel quite comfortable, as we had plenty of house room. This room required a good deal of furniture to make it any way decent, without extravagance, and we were obliged to buy such things as were really necessary, which did not seem much like getting out of debt, but still plunging in deeper and deeper. Yet my creditors were so generous as seldom or ever to call upon me when I was unprepared to meet them.

The first day of June, some gentlemen came and went up the mountains. They had rather a fatiguing time of it, as we had not cleared the path of windfalls which had fallen the preceding winter, and it was excessively warm in the woods, the thermometer standing at ninety-five degrees, and on the summit at sixty degrees. Heat so excessive is seldom experienced here. Notwithstanding, however, the extreme labor which we had to encounter, we felt ourselves amply rewarded by the clouds which enveloped the summit. The clouds on the top occasionally broke away and gave us beautiful views; others appearing between the mountains around us, now rolling up their sides, and now descending into the valley beneath, forming a magnificent prospect. [It is oftentimes that those who climb to the summit are much better satisfied with a storm than they are with a clear sky.] As I have made some extracts from the visitor's album, I will make a few more to show the difference of the weather and the different descriptions given by them, as they come in course, not all, but only those which I think will be interesting for those who have never been here, so that they can form some idea of the place.

July 12th, two gentlemen and a small boy came and ascended the hill unattended by a guide; they went within three-quarters of a mile of the top when they were overtaken by a thunder storm. One of them with the boy returned to the camp, while the other persevered and reached the summit. Mr. Hibbard, one of the gentlemen spoken of, gives the following account of his ascension.[3]

In the aforesaid excursion, I, the said Hibbard, with precipitancy, ascended the mountain and reached the summit within three or four hundred feet, when I was overtaken with a thick cloudy vapor, which rushed on with awful majesty, unmolested in its course even by the mountain itself, and so completely beclouded my way that it was with difficulty I reached the summit. I then concluded to descend to the camp, but was met by the cloud, which shot forth vivid lightning all around me. It was then dark, and I made my way for the tent on the summit, and made myself as comfortable as I could through the night, but suffered some with cold.

The following lines were afterward appended by M. F. M. Waterford Jr.:

> Whoe'er thou art, go view the White Mountains,
> Their cloud cap't tops and crystal fountains;
> Ascend and breathe the healthy mountain air,
> And view the prospect spread so wide and fair—
> Then view the Notch, my friend, return and tell,
> Could you have spent your time and cash so well?

The evening before, the view was grand and sublime.

The same afternoon, a party from the Columbian Academy, with their instructor, Rev. S. R. Hall, came, and at six o'clock in the evening set out, intending to reach the camp that night, but they were overtaken by the storm before mentioned; and I make use of their language to describe it.

> The members of the Columbian Academy proceeded at a very late hour, six o'clock p.m., from E. A. Crawford's and were overtaken with a severe thunder shower before we arrived at the first camp, three miles distant, and there was darkness *impenetrable*. We were obliged to camp in an old camp, wet, cold, and uncomfortable, but we took no cold; started at three o'clock and arrived at the other camp, where we obtained fire and soon had a comfortable breakfast. We then went toward the top of Mount Washington and found it covered with impenetrable fog and clouds. We returned pleased but disappointed.

July 27th, four gentlemen came from different parts of the country, and I went with them on their excursion. We started, and staid overnight at the camp; early the next morning we went up Mount Washington and there enjoyed a noble prospect. On our way home, two of them and myself determined to fish, and after we had arrived at the right place, we turned out and went to the river, while the other two proceeded toward home. [The visitors and sportsmen at that time were not as numerous as at the present day, and the streams taking their rise about the mountains were filled with the speckled trout, the prettiest fish of the finny tribe.] Here we commenced our work, and as fast as we could put in a hook, the trout caught it. One of the party had three hooks attached to his line and frequently caught three at a time, but the bushes were so thick here that they would get tangled and pester him. I told him I could beat him in taking them; for I could put in and take one at a time and get them faster than he could. He came to the same conclusion and accordingly took off all his hooks but one. We had sport enough until satisfied I could carry no more home, and then we left off. We caught in a short time one hundred and thirty-five trout, as many as I could stow in my provision sack, then went home with a plenty of this kind of food to last during their stay, which was enjoyed with equal pleasure as when we were taking them.

About this time a botanist[4] came, who was making a collection of the plants of the White Mountains, as he could obtain here some rare ones such as are not to be found elsewhere in America. I accompanied him in some of his tours around the mountains, and learned the different plants and names and the different places where they grew. He went three times up and around the hills, and staid some weeks with us. In one of his excursions, he was accompanied by three gentlemen and a guide; and the following description of the excursion was given by one of the party.

Left Mr. Crawford's house at seven o'clock a.m., and reached the summit at one o'clock p.m. In the afternoon we were governed by the botanist and his guide. We concluded to camp on the summit and accordingly stowed ourselves away upon the moss on the lee side of a rock, without fire or candles, shivering

and shaking in the mountain breeze like aspen leaves freezing
with cold, the thermometer standing at sunrise at thirty-eight
degrees. In the morning, two of them descended to the camp,
while the botanist, in company with the other, coasted along by
Blue Pond and Mount Munroe, and descended the mountain
by the most villainous break-neck route of the Amanoosuc. God
help the poor wight who attempts that route, as we did. And
now, gentle reader, Heaven bless you and preserve your goings
forth forevermore. Good day.

On the 4th of July, 1825, I think it was, but I may be
mistaken in the exact time, although I was not concerned
in the affair which then took place, a party from Jackson
came up on the other side of the hills, and after enjoying
the prospect as much as they chose, and using the spirit
which we had left there in bottles—which I justified them
in doing, but did not justify them in carrying away the
bottles, which belonged to mother—robbed the hills of the
brass plate, my sheet lead, and everything left there by our
friends, carrying all away. The lead, I was told, was run
into balls; the bottles, of course, were useful; but what use
they could make of the brass, with the Latin inscription
thereon, I am not able to say. But one thing I know, it
discovered a thievish disposition to take things which did
not belong to them and could not do them any good,
things which had been placed there with care and were expected to remain, and would undoubtedly have remained
but for these mischievous persons who did not understand
what belonged to good manners. I have felt myself con-
demned for not prosecuting them, as they ought to have
been chastised and dealt with in a manner according to
their deserts. They were found out, and promised to return the things they had purloined; and that was all they
ever did about it; but the names are known, and their
deeds are registered.

In August, a gentleman came from Boston, attended by his sister. She had made every suitable preparation before leaving home, and was determined to ascend the mountain, although she had been tried to be discouraged on her way by all who knew her intentions, yet she was not so easily turned, she did not mean that there should be anything lacking in a good will. She desired Mrs. Crawford to go with her, and as she had been for a long time anxious to go, I consented,[5] and in the afternoon, having everything in readiness at four o'clock, we started. We rode to the woods, and, each taking a cane, pursued our journey. We walked that night nearly six miles, and arrived at the camp in good season, with a tolerable prospect for the next day. Here all spent the night well, and early in the morning left for the mountain, but before we had got up fairly out of the woods, there came on a fog with a thick mist of rain; this was a great disappointment to us. A council was held, and we agreed to return to the camp and there wait for another day. We accordingly descended to the camp and spent the remainder of the day; in the night it all cleared away, and the next morning, in good season, we were on the summit. How delightful! Now the sun had risen, and as the rain had laid the smoke, the air was perfectly clear and warm, not a cloud nor a vapor to be seen. We could look in every direction and view the works of nature as they lay spread before us; could see towns and villages in the distance, and so clear was the atmosphere that we could distinguish one house from another; but should I attempt to describe the scenery, my pen would fail for want of language to express my ideas of the grandeur of the place. The butterfly was here, busily employed like ourselves, but, perhaps, not in the same way. I have here seen, seemingly, being a mile in the air and a mile above vegetation, squirrels and mice near the top of this hill, and large flocks of ravens, ducks, pigeons, robins, and various other birds fly over and around; a flying squirrel was once caught here, and also a rabbit; partridges are found in the vicinity, and insects of various kinds. [A few winters since, a wild-cat passed the winter in one of the "Tip-Top" houses, having entered and took possession after the summer company had ceased to go up.] After staying a sufficient length of time, we all started for home. Mrs. Crawford went and returned without any assistance, excepting in descending what is called Jacob's Ladder,[6] where I assisted her a short distance. We arrived at the camp, and taking some refreshment, proceeded home, where we arrived about six o'clock. The ladies considered themselves richly paid for their trouble and fatigue, walking nearly eighteen miles. This was the second party of ladies which ascended the mountains; never after this did we persuade ladies to follow their example, but discouraged them whenever we could, endeavoring to prevent them from attempting it, as we thought it too much of an undertaking; but when they became decided and must go, we did all we could to assist them.

The appended extract gives a description of the tour.

The weather was tolerably clear, many clouds floating about, but not so as to obscure the sun. The wind, blowing keen and very strong, prevented our stay longer than half an hour on the top. The view, of course, is very extensive and presents a great sameness on every side; barren and bleak, innumerable hills, many ponds, and the Green Mountains may be discerned in the more distant view. The river Amanoosuc presents one of the most pleasing objects, in its descent from Blue Pond, forming a sheet of silver down the mountain, and winding its serpentined course in the valley. This, contrasted with the deep shade of the pines and other trees, in some degree relieves the eye. Several small streams uniting their waters with this river soon make a sufficient body for trout fishing, many trout of a small size being caught in it. The weather improved on our descent, and after amusing ourselves to our notice, we returned about six o'clock, took supper and again rested all night in the camp, and the next morning arrived at Mr. Crawford's to breakfast.

I will omit making any more extracts, but will insert fragments of the remaining album (much being lost), and return to what transpired at home, according to my own knowledge. The following is transcribed from the album, being written there in the handwriting of Dr. Park.

August 27, 1825, John Park, Mrs. Park, Louisa Jane Park, John C. Park, and Mary Ann Park, of Boston, Mass., arrived at Mr. Crawford's with the intention of ascending Mount Washington. Unfortunately for us, Mr. Crawford had left home a few hours before we arrived, for Lancaster, and was not expected to return until the evening of the next day. Being limited as to time, and the mountains appearing clear, except a little bluish smoke, we determined to proceed on our visit. On the 28th, at two o'clock p.m., we set out with a young man for our guide (Mr. William Howe); took the carriage down to the field about a mile and a half from the house, where we were to enter the woods.

In justice to Mrs. Crawford, I must here mention that beside all her civilities she added the very friendly offer to attend the ladies to the top of the mountain, and expressed the most kind anxiety for them. After a walk, not very fatiguing, and, to us, in many parts, romantic and pleasant, we arrived at the camp twenty minutes before seven. Here Mr. Howe made us a roaring fire, prepared us supper, and all of us, sachems and squaws, betook ourselves to the apartment alloted to us. About midnight it began to rain furiously, but as the clouds came from the west we were still in hopes of a clear day. In the morning clouds were flying thick, but as blue sky was occasionally visible, we concluded to ascend, and, after breakfast, took our departure from the camp, ten minutes past seven, on the morning of the 29th. Hitherto the path had been on a general but moderate ascent. The camp is on the Amanoosuc, and on quitting it, we began immediately to ascend the steep, here making an angle of 45 degrees. To be particular would be tedious. The task is excessively laborious; for ladies, though not impracticable, it is too severe. Having been joined at the camp by our driver, Batchelder, each lady had an assistant, and though after passing the woods and bushy region the wind became very fresh, we all continued to ascend, scrambling over the cliffs for some time. At last, exhausted by fatigue and coming to a shelf of rocks which appeared more than usual steep and difficult, Mrs. Park and my daughter Mary Ann concluded it impossible to proceed. Unpleasant as it was to separate so near the summit, for we were now within three quarters of a mile from the apex, we saw no other plan; and, lodging Mrs. Park and Mary Ann in a cleft between large rocks where they would be in some degree sheltered from the wind, we proceeded, my daughter Louisa Jane having Mr. Howe to support her on one side and Batchelder on the other. It was a desperate business; the wind grew more violent every step we ascended, and the fog or cloud which enveloped us was wet as rain. At twenty-five minutes past ten we reached the top in the midst of a dismal hurricane —no prospect—but certainly our situation partook much of the sublime, from our known elevation, the desolation around us, and the horrors of the tempest.

I have experienced gales in the Gulf Stream, tempests off Cape Hatteras, tornadoes in the West Indies, and been surrounded by water spouts in the Gulf of Mexico, but I never saw anything more furious or more dreadful than this. I staid on the top but five minutes, anxious for those whom we had left. In less than half of an hour, I found them safe, though cold and anxious. The rest of our party soon arrived, and taking a little refreshment, we began to descend together. Soon after we left the regions of barrenness and desolation and entered the woods, we were met by Mr. Crawford himself, who had kindly come out to see what might be our situation. We arrived safe and well at the encampment at fifteen minutes after one, took a little refreshment, and continued our return to Mr. Crawford's, where we arrived precisely at six o'clock p.m., having been absent about twenty-eight hours.

Gentlemen, there is nothing in the ascent of Mount Washington that you need dread. Ladies, give up all thoughts of it; but if you are resolved, let the season be mild, consult Mr. Crawford as to the prospects of the weather, and with every precaution, you will still find it, *for you*, a tremendous undertaking.

Though we were disappointed after all we had read and heard in not having Mr. Crawford for our guide, yet we had no reason to complain. Mr. Howe, who conducted us, will be found a faithful and obliging young man. Of Mr. and Mrs. Crawford's kindness and attention during our short stay here, we have ample reason to join in the common report of all travelers.[7]

In September, the same year, a small party of gentlemen and three ladies came to visit the mountains, and I went with them. We staid at the camp over night; next day we went up the hill and back again to the camp with little trouble or fatigue. After this, when walking on a more level way, one of the ladies became lame in her ankles, and it was with difficulty she could walk. I then took off the bundle of clothes from my back and made a good cushion of them and placed them on my right shoulder, took my hat in my left hand; the gentlemen then sat her upon my right shoulder, and I brought her some miles in this way quite well. I have brought gentlemen along in a similar way when they thought they could go no further.

The following is another extract from the album:

When we started in the morning, we were fearful of rain, but the weather was good, and the temperature of the air comparatively warm on the summit. Our prospect but ill repaid us the fatigue of ascending, as the atmosphere was smoky. After remaining on the summit for more than an hour, and singing "Old Hundred," in which the whole party joined, at half past eleven o'clock, we began to descend, and reached the camp in two hours and a half. Here the party rested and refreshed about an hour; left the camp and arrived at Mr. Crawford's at seven o'clock in the evening. As the ladies of our party made a third of the number who

have reached the summit of Mount Washington, something
may be expected to be said of them and of the practicability of
the ascent for ladies. Miss Harriet C. Woodward performed the
ascent and descent of the mountain and the walk from the camp
to Mr. Crawford's with much less fatigue than could have been
expected. Miss Lawrence suffered a little more. Miss Elizabeth
Woodward supported the ascent and descent to the camp tolerably well, but became excessively fatigued and lame during
the return walk from the camp to Mr. Crawford's, and had it
not been for the kind and humane attention and assistance of
Mr. C., which we here record with much gratitude, would
scarcely have been able to have reached Mr. C.'s. In conclusion,
could ladies be carried and find a little more comfortable accommodations on the mountains, the ascent of Mount Washington, even, would be a comparatively easy achievement. As it
is, ladies, do not attempt it; at least, *never but in fair weather*.
Of Mr. Crawford's kindness and humanity nothing need be
said; all who visit the mountain will be satisfied with it.

Getting tired of carrying blankets every time we went
up this mountain, and not being able to leave them in
safety on account of the mice and squirrels, for they would
make holes in them unless we hung them on a tree, and
then they were exposed to the weather, sometime in the
forepart of the summer I bought a sufficient quantity of
sheet-iron and made a chest that would hold ten bushels,
apparently large enough for the man who carried it to lie
down and rest himself in. This we placed at the camp and
there made a deposit for all things that might be left there.
We had eleven blankets and cooking untensils for cooking
a good warm meal, and would frequently add to the variety by a dish of trout, which could be caught but a few
rods from the camp. These I could cook to a charm, much
better than an old experienced cook in a city hotel could
—at least, they tasted much better here than there. I had
plenty of good salt pork to cook them with, and that is the

very thing that gives them a relish; and fatigue would never fail of giving us good appetites. Afterward I made my tea and then could drink it in clean fresh-washed cups. I had here every convenience for doing all this work. I was presented with a box of tin-ware of a superior quality from the before mentioned botanist, containing an apparatus sufficient for a number to eat and drink with together; and on the corner of the iron chest I would sometimes put birch bark from a tree and spread it as a substitute for a cloth, and in this way I have enjoyed many a good meal with my friends.

We had two camps built, and they stood facing each other, and there was a good fire in the middle. The wood we cut from six to eight feet in length and rolled it together, any way or size we could manage, and when one pile burnt out we would put another on, and thus kept a good fire through the night. One camp was for ladies, and the other for gentlemen. For beds we took a large quantity of spruce and hemlock boughs and laid them down, spread our blankets upon them, and this would make a healthy bed. To secure the ladies, we would make a blanket curtain in front of their camp, and they were entirely by themselves. Now the untiring mosquito would sing to us constantly and every now and then would stop and taste a little.[8]

CHAPTER VIII

———

The storm of 1826.
The great slide from the mountains.
The destruction of the Willey family.
Mr. Crawford's loss.

SINGULAR as it may appear, not a person has ever been known to take cold in camping upon the summit, previous to the erection of the Tip-Top houses. Mr. Crawford, frequently, during his stay at the mountains, received letters from various invalids saying their health was much improved by their visits. Even at the present day, seldom can a person retire to rest upon the beds in the summit house without finding a damp blanket to get into; yet one always feels refreshed in the morning without any symptoms of having taken a cold.][1]

Now we were in trouble again, there being a complaint for want of a shed and more stable room. The winter of 1826 was at hand with a great deal to do. After having done other necessary business, I went to hauling boards and shingles from the same short distance of twelve miles, only up through the Notch. My father had put him up a new saw-mill, and I could get boards from there now better than from anywhere else, but it was some trouble to draw them up the Notch hills. Some perhaps think this a heavy job, but when a thing is undertaken in good earnest, it is soon over; so with this job. In the spring I hired men and went to work and soon had timber prepared for a stable sixty feet by forty, and a shed to stand between the old stable and the new one, fifty feet by forty, which accommodated both stables, and the whole length of these buildings was nearly one hundred and fifty feet, in a straight line, facing the road. The outside of these buildings was nearly finished when a stop was put to all business in consequence of the great rain, which you will soon find recorded.[2]

In June, [1826,] as my father with a number of men was at work repairing the turnpike road through the Notch, there came on a heavy rain, and they were obliged to leave their work and retire to the house, then occupied by the worthy Willey family, and it rained very hard. While there they saw on the west side of the road a small movement of rocks and earth coming down the hill, and it took all before it. They saw, likewise, whole trees coming down, standing upright, for ten rods together, before they would tip over—the whole still moving slowly on, making its way until it had crossed the road and then on a level surface some distance before it stopped. This grand and awful sight frightened the timid family very much, and Mrs. Willey proposed to have the horses harnessed and go to my father's, but the old gentleman told her not to be alarmed, as he said they were much safer there than they would be in the road; for, said he, there may be other difficulties in the way, like the one just described, or the swollen waters may have carried away some of the bridges and they could not be crossed; and after some reasoning with her in this way she was pacified and remained safely. The next day, as the storm had abated, they set about removing the burden from the road, which required much trouble and labor. This seemed to be a warning and it appeared so to them. Mr. Willey had looked round and about the mountains and tried to find out a safer place than the one they then occupied; and, having satisfied himself, as he thought, placed a good tight cart-body in such a manner as would secure them from the weather in case a similar thing should occur, as visitors had advised them to leave the place as they were anxious for their safety; and he, it appeared, was fearful, or he would not have made this effort. But there is an overruling God who knows all things and causes all things to happen for the best, although we short-sighted mortals cannot comprehend them. Had they taken the advice of St. Paul and all abode in the ship, they might have been saved; but this was not to be their case— they were suffered to perish.

August 26th, there came a party from the West to ascend the mountain, but as the wind had been blowing from the south for several days, I advised them not to go that afternoon, but they said their time was limited and they must proceed. Everything necessary for the expedition being put in readiness, we all, like so many good soldiers, with our staves in our hands, set forward at six o'clock and arrived at the camp at ten o'clock; and I with my knife and flint struck fire, which caught in a piece of dry punk which I carried for that purpose, and from that I could make a large fire. This was the only way we had in those days of obtaining fire. [The old-fashioned steel or jack-knife and flint were necessary appendages in those days in performing camp duty.] After my performing the duties of a cook and house maid, we sat down in the humble situation of Indians, not having the convenience of chairs, and told stories till the time for rest.[3] The wind still continued to blow from the south. In the morning, about four o'clock, it commenced raining, which prevented their hopes of ascending the mountain that day, and not having provisions for another day, and they being unwilling now to give it up when they had got so near, a meeting was called and it was unanimously agreed that I should go home and get new supplies and then return to them again. I obeyed their commands, shouldered my empty pack, took my leave of them and returned; but, as the rain was falling so fast, and the mud collected about my feet, my progress was slow and wearisome. I at length got home, and being tired and my brother Thomas being there, I desired him to take my place, which he cheerfully consented to do, and in a short time he was laden and set forward; and when arriving at the camp, the party was holding a council as to what was to be done, for the rain had fallen so fast and steadily that it had entirely extinguished the fire. They consulted Thomas upon the matter to know if they had time to get in. He told them that to remain there would be very unpleasant, as they must suffer with the wet and cold, not considering danger, but if they would go as fast as they could, they might reach the house. Each taking a little refreshment in his hands, and having the precaution to take the axe with them, set off in full speed, and when they came to a swollen stream which they could not ford, Thomas would, with his axe, fell a tree for a bridge, and then they would walk over. They got along tolerably well until they came to a large branch, which came from the Notch. This was full and raging, and they had some difficulty to find a tree that would reach to the opposite bank, but at length succeeded in finding one, and they all got safely over, and those who could not walk, crawled along, holding on by the limbs; and when they came to the main stream, the water had risen and come into the road for several rods, and when they crossed the bridge it trembled under their feet. They all arrived in safety about eight o'clock in the evening, when they were welcomed by two large fires to dry themselves. Here they took off their wet garments, and those that had not a change of their own put on mine and went to bed, while we sat up to dry theirs. At eleven o'clock we had a clearing up shower, and it seemed as though the windows of heaven were opened and the rain came down almost in streams. It did not, however, last long before it all cleared away and became a perfect calm. The next morning we were awakened by our little boy coming into the room and saying, "Father, the earth is nearly covered with water, and the hogs are swimming for life." I arose immediately and went to their rescue. I waded into the water and pulled away the fence, and they swam to land. What a sight! The sun rose clear; not a cloud nor a vapor was to be seen; all was still and silent excepting the rushing sound of the water as it poured down the hills [leaping over huge precipices and centering in one vast ocean in the valley beneath.] The whole interval was covered with water a distance of over two hundred acres of land, to be seen when standing on the little hill which has been named and called Giant's Grave, just back of the stable, where the house used to stand that was burnt. After standing here a short time, I saw the fog arise in different places on the water, and it formed a beautiful sight. The bridge, which had so lately been crossed, had come down and taken with it ninety feet of shed which was attached to the barn that escaped the fire in 1818. Fourteen sheep that were under it were drowned, and those which escaped looked as though they had been washed in a mud puddle. The water came within eighteen inches of the door in the house and a strong current was running between the house and stable. It came up under the shed and underneath the new stable and carried away timber and wood, passed by the west corner of the house, and moved a wagon which stood in its course.

Now the safety of my father and of the Willey family occupied our minds, but there was no way to find out their situation. At or near the middle of the day (Tuesday), there came a traveler on foot who was desirous of going down the Notch that night, as he said his business was urgent and he must, if possible, go through. I told him to be patient, as the water was then falling fast, and as soon as it should fall and I could swim a horse, I would carry him over the river. Owing to the narrowness of the intervals between the mountains here, when it begins to fall it soon drains away, and at four o'clock I mounted a large strong horse, took the traveler on behind, swam the river, and landed him safely on the other side and returned. He made the best of his way down to the Notch house and arrived there just before dark. He found the house deserted by every living creature excepting the faithful dog, and he was unwilling at first to admit the stranger. He at length became friendly and acquainted. On going to the barn he found it had been touched by an avalanche and fallen in. The two horses that were in it were both killed, and the oxen confined under the broken timber tied in their stalls. These he set at liberty after finding an axe and cutting away the timber; they were lame but soon got over it. What must have been the feelings of this lonely traveler while occupying this deserted house, finding doors opened and bed and clothes as though they had been left in a hurry, bible open and lying on the table as if it had lately been read? He went round the house and prepared for himself a supper and partook of it alone except the company of the dog, who seemed hungry like himself; then quietly lay down in one of these open deserted beds and consoled himself by thinking the family had made their escape and gone down to my father's. Early the next morning he proceeded on his way and he had some difficulty in getting across some places, as the earth and water were mixed together and made a complete quagmire. He succeeded in getting to Father's, but could obtain no information of the unfortunate family, [and he therefore concluded that they must all have been buried beneath the slide.] He told this story as he went down through Bartlett and Conway, and the news soon spread.

On Wednesday the waters had subsided so much that we could ford the Amanoosuc river with a horse and wagon, and some of the time-limited party agreed to try the ground over again; so they, with the addition of another small party who came from the West on Tuesday, with Thomas for guide, again set out, while I, with a gentleman from Connecticut, went toward the Notch. After traveling a distance of two miles in a wagon, we were obliged to leave it and take to our feet. We now found the road in some places entirely demolished and, seemingly, on a level surface; a crossway which had been laid down for many years and firmly covered with dirt—that to the eye of human reason it would be impossible to move—taken up, and every log had been disturbed and laid in different directions. On going still a little further, we found a gulf in the middle of the road, in some places ten feet deep and twenty rods in length. The rest of the road my pen would fail should I attempt to describe it; suffice it to say, I could hardly believe my own eyes, the water having made such destruction. Now, when within a short distance of the house, I found the cows with their bags filled with milk, and from their appearance, they had not been milked for some days. My heart sickened as I thought what had happened to the inmates of the house. We went in and there found no living person and the house in the situation just described. I was going down to my father's to seek them out, but the gentleman with me would not let me go, for he said he could not find his way back alone, and I must return with him. We set out and arrived home at four o'clock in the afternoon.

I could not be satisfied about the absent family and again returned, and when I got back to the house found a number of the neighbors had assembled, and no information concerning them could be obtained. My feelings were such that I could not remain there during the night, although a younger brother of mine, being one of the company, almost laid violent hands upon me to compel me to stay, fearing some accident might befall me, as I should have to feel my way through the Notch on my hands and knees, for the water had in the narrowest place in the Notch taken out the rocks which had been beat in from the ledge above to make the road, and carried them into the gulf below and made a hole or gulf twenty feet deep, and it was difficult, if not dangerous, to get through in the night, as all those who visited this scene of desolation will bear testimony to; but my mind was fixed and unchangeable, and I would not be prevailed on to stay. I started and groped my way home in the dark, where I arrived at ten o'clock in the evening. Here I found that the party from the mountain had arrived; as they had nowhere to stay, they were obliged to come in that night. Now we began to relate our discoveries. They had much difficulty in finding their way, as the water had made as bad work with their path as it had done with the road, in proportion to its length. The water had risen and carried away every particle of the camp and all my furniture there. The party seemed thankful that they, on Monday, had made their escape. What must have been their fortune had they remained there? They must have shared the same fate the Willey family did, or suffered a great deal with fear, wet, cold, and hunger, for it would have been impossible for them to have come in until Wednesday, and their provisions must have been all gone, if not lost, on Monday night. It seemed really a providential thing in their being saved. No part of the iron chest was ever found, or anything it contained, excepting a few pieces of blanket that were caught on bushes in different places down the river.

The next morning our friends, with gratitude, left us; and we had the same grateful feelings toward them, wishing each other good luck.

The same day (Thursday) before I had time to look about me and learn the situation of my farm and estimate the loss I had sustained, the friends of the Willey family had come up to the deserted house and sent for me. At first I said I could not go down, but being advised to, I went. When I got there, on seeing the friends of that well-beloved family, and having been acquainted with them for many years, my heart was full and my tongue refused utterance, and I could not for a considerable length of time speak to one of them, and could only express the regard I had for them in pressing their hands and giving full vent to my tears. This was the second time my eyes were wet with tears since grown to manhood. The other time was when my family was in that destitute situation. Diligent search being made for them, and no traces to be found until night, the attention of the people was attracted by the flies as they were passing and repassing underneath

a large pile of floodwood. They now began to haul away
the rubbish and at length found Mr. and Mrs. Willey, Mr.
Allen, the hired man, and the youngest child not far distant from each other. These were taken up, broken and
mangled, as must naturally be expected, and were placed
in coffins. The next day they were interred on a piece of
ground near the house, there to remain until winter. Saturday, the other hired man was found and interred, and
on Sunday the eldest daughter was found, some way from
where the others were, across the river; and it was said her
countenance was fair and pleasant, not a bruise or a mark
was discovered upon her. It was supposed she was
drowned. She had only a handkerchief around her waist,
supposed to have been put there for someone to lead her
by. This girl was not far from twelve years of age. She had
acquired a good education,[4] considering her advantages,
and she seemed more like a gentleman's daughter, of fashion and affluence, than the daughter of one who had located himself in the midst of the mountains. It is said the
earliest flowers are the soonest plucked, and this seems to
be the case with this young, interesting family; the rest of
the children were not inferior to the eldest, considering
their age. In this singular act of Providence, there were
nine taken from time into eternity, four adult persons and
five children. It should remind us, we who are living, to "be
also ready, for in such an hour as ye think not, the Son of
Man cometh." It was a providential thing, said Zara Cutler, Esq., who was present afterward, that the house itself
was saved, so near came the overwhelming avalanche. The
length of the slides are several miles down the side of the
mountain. The other three children, one daughter and
two sons, have never to this day been found; not even a
bone has ever been picked up or discovered. It is supposed

they must have been buried deep underneath an avalanche. [What must have been the feelings of that family as they rushed from the house under the darkness of night, knowing not where to flee for safety from the mighty torrent of earth and water which was hurrying itself along down into the valley beneath?]

Mr. and Mrs. Willey sustained good and respectable characters, and were in good standing among the Christians in Conway, where they belonged.[5] They were remarkable for their charities and kindness toward others, and commanded the respect of travelers and all who knew them. Much more could be said in their favor, but it would be superfluous to add.[6] Suffice it to remark that the whole intention of their lives was to live humbly, walk uprightly, deal justly with all, speak evil of none.

There came a large slide down back of the house in a direction to take the house with it, and when within ten or fifteen rods of the house it came against a solid ledge of rock and there stopped and separated, one on either side of the house, taking the stable on one side, and the family on the other, or they might have got to the rendezvous; but there is no certainty which of these divisions overtook them, as they were buried partly by the three slides which had come together eighty rods from the house; the two that separated back of the house here met, and a still larger one had come down in the place where Mr. Willey had hunted out a safe refuge. When the slide was coming down and separating, it had great quantities of timber with it, [turned over the large boulders and set them in motion down the mountain.] One log, six feet long and two feet through, still kept its course and came within three feet of the house, but fortunately it was stopped by coming against a brick, where it rested; the ends of trees were torn

up and looked similar to an old peeled birch broom. The
whole valley, which was once covered with beautiful green
grass, was now a complete quagmire, exhibiting nothing
but ruins of the mountains, heaps of timber, large rocks,
sand, and gravel. All was dismal and desolate. [Even the
faithful dog seemed to partake of the sympathy, and after
trying to arouse by his moanings a neighboring family but
without success, it is said, he soon disappeared from the
spot and was never heard from after.] For a monument, I
wrote with a piece of red chalk on a planed board this
inscription:

THE FAMILY FOUND HERE.

I nailed it to a dead tree which was standing near the
place where they were found; but it has since been taken
away by some of the occupants of the house and used for
fuel.[7]

But to return to my own affairs at home. Fences mostly
gone, farm in some places covered so deeply with sand and
gravel that it was ruined, and, on the interval, floodwood
was piled in great and immense quantities in different
places all over it. The bridge now lay in pieces all around
the meadow, and the shed also; there was a large field of
oats just ready to harvest, from which I think I would have
had four or six hundred bushels, which was destroyed;
also, some hay in the field. My actual loss at this time was
more than one thousand dollars, and truly things looked
rather unfavorable. After the fire, we had worked hard and
economized closely to live and pay our former dues, in
which we made slow progress. As it was necessary for the
benefit of the public to buy so many things which we could
not get along without, I could do but little toward taking
up my old notes, but still I must persevere and keep doing
while the day lasted, and I thought no man would be

punished for being unfortunate. Therefore, taking these things into consideration, I would still continue to do the best I could and trust the event. My father suffered still more than myself. The best part of his farm was entirely destroyed. A new saw mill, which he had just put up, and a great number of logs and boards were swept away together into the sand; fences on the interval were all gone; twenty-eight sheep were drowned, and considerable grain which was in the field was swept away. The water rose on the outside of the house twenty-two inches, and ran through the whole house on the lower floors and swept out the coals and ashes from the fireplace. They had lighted candles, which were placed in the windows, and my mother took down a pole which she used as a clothes pole and stood at a window near the corner of the house when the current ran swift, and would push away the timber and other stuff that came down against the house to keep it from collecting in a great body, as she thought it might jam up and sweep away the house, for the water was rising fast. And while thus engaged, she was distressed by the cries of the poor bleating and drowning sheep that would pass by in the flood and seemed to cry for help, but none could be afforded.

My father at this time was from home, and but few of the family were there, so they made the best they could of it. This came on so suddenly and unexpectedly that almost everything in the cellar was ruined, and a part of the wall fell in.

This loss of my father's property, which he had accumulated only by the sweat of his brow, was so great that he will never be likely to regain it. Many suffered more or less who lived on this wild and uncultivated stream, as far as Saco.

We had now a difficulty which seemed almost insur-
mountable. The road in many places was entirely gone;
the bridges, the whole length of the turnpike excepting
two, a distance of seventeen miles, gone; the directors
came and looked at it and found it would take a large sum
to repair it. The good people of Portland, however, to encourage us, raised fifteen hundred dollars to help us with;
it was put into the hands of Nathan Kinsman, Esq., to see
it well laid out. The directors voted to raise an assessment
on the shares, to make up the balance; and that, with some
other assistance, was divided into jobs and let out, and we
all went to work; and, as it was said, the sun shone so short
a time in this Notch, that the hardy New Hampshire boys
made up their hours by moonlight.

CHAPTER IX[1]

———

*Search for minerals. The sad tale of Nancy.
Nancy's Brook. Trip to the summit.
Deep snows. Great rains. Trapping.*

WE got along much better with this work than we expected. We were favored with good weather and had
a decent sleigh path for the winter. This great and wonderful catastrophe which happened among the mountains
caused a great many to visit the place that fall. Among
others there came two gentlemen for the purpose of going
up to the mountain and visiting the slides to ascertain the
qualities of naked mountains, as they were in search of
minerals. We found on the west side of Mount Pleasant
the largest slide; it appeared one thousand acres in dimen-
sion had slid off and rested in the valley below. We wandered about, looking at the wonderful works of God, until
night overtook us, and then on a ridge of the hill near the
Amanoosuc, by the side of a large pile of floodwood, I
built a camp, or wigwam, which was sufficiently large for
us then. I cut my wood, struck a fire, and we each took our
blanket and retired to rest. As might be expected, the
night at this season of the year, was long and cold; a thick
mist of rain came on, and our quarters being small, they
complained of the cold and want of room. I arose, renewed
my fire, and spread my blanket on them, and retired, myself, to a thick fir tree, under whose boughs I took shelter
and soon fell asleep; being very tired, and now having

plenty of room, and feeling my companions were more comfortable, I slept till morning. When I returned to my companions they were glad to see the light of another day. I have been over and around the mountains in almost every direction with botanists and with mineralogists. I have been up and down all the slides of any magnitude and have taken pains to find out if there were any minerals of value there, but have never as yet found any of consequence.

It has been supposed by some that there were valuable mines somewhere about the mountains. I have searched for these also, but found none. I recollect a number of years ago, when quite a boy, some persons had been up on the hills and said they had found a golden treasure, or carbuncle, which they said was under a large shelving rock and would be difficult to obtain for they might fall and be dashed to pieces.[2] Moreover, they thought it was guarded by an evil spirit, supposing that it had been placed there by the Indians, and that they had killed one of their number and left him to guard the treasure, which some credulous, superstitious persons believed, and they got my father to engage to go and search for it. Providing themselves with everything necessary for the business and a sufficient number of good men and a minister well qualified to lay the evil spirit, they set out in good earnest and high spirits, anticipating with pleasure how rich they should be in coming home laden with gold; that is, if they should have the good luck to find it. They set out and went up Dry river, and had hard work to find their way through the thickets and over the hills, where they made diligent search for a number of days, with some of the former men spoken of for guides, but they could not find the place again, or anything that seemed to be like it, and worn out with fatigue and disappointment, they returned. Never since, to my knowledge, has anyone found that wonderful place again, or been troubled with the mountain spirit.

I have heard it said by the people of Portsmouth that when children were at play and happened to fall out with each other, the worst punishment they could inflict upon their mates was to wish them up at the White Hills, as that was considered the worst place in the world by them. Perhaps their minds had been affected by the story of Nancy, who perished in the woods in attempting to follow her lover.[3] She had been at work in Jefferson for Colonel Whipple when the heart of this honest girl was won by a servant of his; as he was going in the fall to Portsmouth, he promised to take her along with him, and after they should arrive there, he would make her his wife. She was honest herself and thought him to be also, and as he had contrived every means to please her in all the domestic concerns in which they were engaged while under the control of the Colonel, she had entrusted him with her money which had been paid her for her labor and went to Lancaster to make preparations for the intended journey. While she was preparing, her lover went away with the Colonel and left her behind. She was immediately informed of his treachery and was determined to pursue him. There had been a deep snow and there was no road, nothing but spotted trees, beside the tracks of the Colonel and her false lover, to follow. When she arrived at Jefferson she was wet with snow which had collected upon her clothes, and was wearied. The men that were there tried to persuade her not to go any further, setting forth the many difficulties she would have to encounter and likewise the danger she would be exposed to in such an undertaking,

through a howling wilderness of thirty miles, without fire
or food. All these entreaties did not move her or alter her
determination; for such was her love, either for the man
upon whom she had placed her affections or the money
she had placed in his hands, that she was inflexible. Having a great opinion of her own ability, in her imagination
she thought, as they had only been gone some hours and
would probably go no further than the Notch that night,
probably camping there, she might, by traveling all night,
overtake them before they started in the morning.[4] In this
she was disappointed; they had left before she arrived; but
from every appearance the fire had not gone out. It may be
inquired how it was known that the fire had not gone out
there? When a fire is made in the woods, it is made of very
large wood, cut and rolled together, and then left to burn,
as was evidently the case here, and there will be brands
left at each end of the fire. These brands she had put together, and they burnt out, as the ashes plainly showed for
themselves when the men found them. She was tired and
worn out with fatigue and hunger, having taken nothing
with her to eat on the way. Yet her passion was not abated,
and she still persevered, thinking she should overtake
them. She went on and got a distance of twenty-two miles
when the men, thinking she was in earnest, followed her.
When she set off in the afternoon, they thought she would
not go far before she would come back, and they waited
until late in the evening, expecting every moment to hear
the sound of her footsteps at the door; but in vain did they
imagine this. They pressed on and found the fire in the
situation just described, which made them think she found
fire to warm her benumbed limbs. Here they rested only a
short time and then proceeded and found her just after
crossing a brook, in a sitting position, with her clothes

frozen upon her, having wet them while crossing the brook, and her head was resting on her hand and cane which had been her support through the woods, and she was frozen to death.

This place is near my father's, and has ever since, from that circumstance, borne the name of Nancy's Brook and Nancy's Hill.

> Now in this volume let me build a tomb
> For Nancy, love's sweet victim, in her bloom.
> Her tragic end, though awful to relate,
> Shows how true love controls a woman's fate!
> Oh! had she early given her heart to God,
> Perhaps she had not felt the chastening rod.
> But let us trust her sins are all forgiven,
> And with her Savior, that she rests in Heaven.
>
>   J. C. N. I.

The reader would perhaps like to know what became of her lover. Shortly after hearing of this, his own conscience was smitten and he became frantic and insane, and was put into the hospital, where he in a few months after died in a most horrible condition. This is a true story, as I have heard it told by those who were knowing to the facts, as related in the above statement.

October 14th, there came a gentleman from Germany to ascend the mountains.[5] I provided him with a good guide, and they set out early in the morning, knowing they must return that evening, as there was no place for them to stay on their way overnight. I waited for their return until nine o'clock in the evening, feeling anxious for them, fearing they might be lost, as there had come down in the flood a large quantity of timber and filled up the path so that it was difficult finding it not far from the entrance of the woods. I did not know but they might be lost in this place,

as it would be dark before they could arrive there, and well
knowing the night must be long, cold, and tedious in
their destitute situation, I took a lantern and my long tin
horn, mounted a horse, and proceeded to the woods,
where I alighted and then commenced blowing the horn,[6]
which was soon answered by the guide. I took my light
and steered toward the sound of his voice; there I found
them completely lost, not more than a quarter of a mile
from the open ground. When they came there it was dark,
and though the guide had been there many times before
and knew the way well, yet the darkness bewildered him
so much that it was in vain he tried to get out, and when
satisfied he could not, he groped his way about in the dark
and had broken some boughs to lie down upon, without a
blanket, and no other covering than the canopy of heaven
to cover them. Destitute of food, and not having the means
of making a fire, they had made up their minds to spend
the night in this uncomfortable situation when the joyful
sound of the horn caught their ears. I soon put them in a
way to get liberated from this place, and when they came
to the horse, I helped the gentleman on his back, and then
we all came home; and a more grateful man than this I
scarce ever saw. When arrived at the house, and finding
his situation changed from that cold and lonesome one to
a good warm fire and supper and the expectation of a good
bed, it almost overcame him.

[The above description shows how necessary it is for
persons ascending the mountains to procure a guide unless well acquainted with a woods life. To prepare fuel for
the night fires and build a camp suitable to protect from
the mountain winds requires experience.]

The winter of 1827 I spent much like the former winter
seasons; buying and laying-in a still larger share of pro-

visions than usual for the benefit of those who should need them while at work on the road, and for the purpose of assisting the weary traveler through the deep snows and over our rough roads.

In the spring I went to work on my mountain road[7] as soon as the ground would permit, and I made a road suitable for a carriage a distance of one and a half miles into the woods. We could now ride in a carriage from my house, three miles, and our custom was at that time to carry visitors to the end of the road, and then return with the carriage and leave them to try their own strength from there up and back, and then we would be ready there on their return to bring them home again. I had intended to work on this road every year, when I could, until I should have completed it to the foot of Mount Washington.

After reading the description given by Dr. Park and the other party of ladies, shortly after their return, and finding their opinion was that it was not exactly fitting for ladies to attempt such an arduous undertaking, all the ladies that visited the mountain were more willing to give up the idea of the ascent, although they had as much curiosity to view and contemplate things not made with hands; and still they, in general, possess an ambition to excell and attain to such noble and romantic acts, for some energy both of mind and body is required to perform such an enterprise. There had never been but four parties of ladies up the mountain since I had come here to live, now ten years past, and I had promised the ladies that whenever I could make a road suitable for them to ride a part or all of the way to the foot of the hill, I would never, in good weather, discourage them from going there, but would go with them myself and assist them wherever it was necessary. I had made a road to ride on part of the way, and ladies began to

take me at my word and this summer began to ascend the
mountain again. Whenever we had more company than
what belonged to any particular party, I would furnish
them with another guide, so that they should not be troubled or hindered in the least; they might go with us or by
themselves, just as the parties chose. I spent this summer
in going up and down the mountain with my friends, visiting the Notch and the desolate Willey House, giving
them as good an account of what took place on that memo-
rable night of the second of August last and answering all
their inquiries as promptly and correctly as my humble
capacity and judgment would allow me to do.

It now became needful for the benefit of the company,
as it increased, to have an establishment at the top of the
Notch,[8] as many wanted to stop there and leave their
horses and pursue their way down the hill on foot to view
the cascades as they come majestically down the hill and
over the rocks and form such a beautiful silvery sight. The
flume, likewise, that is curiously cut out by nature through
a solid rock, the avalanches, and then the Willey House,
etc. On their return they needed refreshment, and having
a disposition to accommodate the public, and feeling a
little self-pride to have another Crawford settled here, to
make up a road, I consulted with my father, and we agreed
to build there and place a brother of mine in the house.
We accordingly made a plan upon the best and most convenient construction we could invent, and, in the fall, prepared timber for a frame one hundred and twenty feet in
length, and thirty-six feet in width. Just as we were about
to raise this, the snow fell so deeply that we were obliged
to give it up for the present time.

I think that it was this fall that a man from Falmouth
had been to Lancaster and bought some fat sheep and

oxen; he had a team of horses and a wagon, and on his
way home as he was coming over Cherry Mountain, it
began to snow. He arrived at my house, where he put up
for the night, and it continued to snow until it had fallen
two feet and over; here he staid until it cleared away, and
then he could not travel with his sheep, the snow was so
deep. I then, with him, began to contrive means to help
him along. We harnessed his horses and put them to a
wagon, the oxen on forward of them; but this did not make
a path sufficient for the sheep to go in. I then harnessed a
horse and drove a wedge into a short, large, round log,
put a chain around this wedge, and led my horse, and this
log made a complete road for them to go in, single file; in
this way, we got along quite well down into the Notch a
little way, when the snow became thin, then he could go
without my assistance. I then left my log, mounted my
horse, and returned home, while the traveler pursued his
journey without suffering much inconvenience from the
snow. It was no uncommon thing for us to have two feet of
snow, while in Bartlett they would not have more than two
inches; as we lived so high in the air, and the mountains
generally attract or hinder the storms, we had snow, while
others, who lived not more than twenty miles distant had
rain and sometimes sunshine; such was the variableness of
the weather where we then lived; still, in the summer we
generally had a good share of good and clear weather, but
spring and fall were the times when we had most of these
sudden changes. Uncle William says that in former days,
when they first went there to live, the snow would sometimes be ten feet deep, and he has seen the time when they
could drive a team of oxen and horses anywhere in the
field on the crust, over stumps and fences, and draw their
wood home from any place they chose, wherever they

The Mount Crawford House and Mount Crawford, from
Oakes' *Scenery of the White Mountains*

The Notch House at the head of the Notch,
from Oakes' *Scenery of the White Mountains*

The Crawford Monument at Fabyans, just off Route 302, from a photograph taken around 1875. The wooden fence has been replaced

could best get it, as this hard crust made a smooth surface for them to go on. Had it not been for this, they could not have got along where they did, because it was rough and stumpy, and from such little circumstances it seems that there is nothing made in vain. I have seen the snow so deep, when I lived there, that it was difficult for men to pass each other with teams when they met, until they had stamped down the snow and made a path for one of them to get out, and then sometimes they would have to unhitch their horses and compel them to turn out, such was the depth of snow; and where there was a crust on it, it was still more difficult. At one time when I was coming home from Portland with a loaded sleigh, when I got up as far as my father's it was snowing, and there I baited my horses; intending to reach home that night, I went on as far as the Notch House and there hired a man to help me up the hill, with two horses; we went on part of the way, but the snow was so deep that his horses would not work, and we were obliged to leave the sleigh and return to the house. I had the precaution to put the tongue of the sleigh upward, and the next morning when I came to where I had left the sleigh, all that I could discover of it was the tongue; this stood upright. The rest of it was entirely covered with the snow, and it was then utterly impossible for me to take it with me, so I there left it. A man happened to be with me, who had staid with me the preceding night and was on his way to Vermont, with an empty single sleigh and a good horse. One of my horses I put on forward of his, and I and the other horse made a track for them to follow; we worked hard half a day to get six miles, such was the quantity of snow that had fallen in a few hours. Other descriptions I could give similar to this, but I do not wish to tire the patience of the reader with more than what is necessary to show the difference between the climate we live in and other climates not far from us, and what difficulties and hardships we had to encounter in this region; but in later years, for some cause, we have not had such quantities of snow and have not been much troubled with its depth, but many times for the want of it.

In the winter, in the beginning of the year 1828, we went to work and bought lumber and had it drawn a distance of seventeen and a half miles. I bought my brick and had to haul them twenty-two miles, which kept us busy through the winter with what other work we had to do. In the spring we collected men and raised these buildings. I hired two joiners, and they went to work on them.

In June, I again worked on my mountain road and then made it passable for a carriage, with what I had done the year before, a distance from my house of about six miles, on which I could carry in a wagon, with two stout horses, seven passengers at a time, and this made it much easier for the traveler, for ladies could go up much easier than they could at any other time before. They went oftener, and I spent the most of this summer in ascending the mountain with my friends at the house, and in fishing and hunting with them as much as they chose, and bestowing every act of kindness on them which I was capable of doing. The joiners, with what other assistance we could afford them, had the outside of these buildings finished and the inside so much done that it was comfortable for the winter. We were still at work when on the 2d day of September we were again visited by a heavy rain, which was as great as the one we had two years before. The water in some places on the Amanoosuc, where the mountains come near together, was higher than in the former freshet. On the Saco it was not so high, yet the other freshet had made the channel of the river so wide that the water flood could pass without being dammed up or stopped in places, as it had been in the former one, therefore it did not occasion so much damage but passed majestically along, taking only what lay in its course. The bridges, which had so lately been built anew, were mostly taken from their places and moved away, but not so far but that some of them could be brought back and put in their former places again. The road was in many places entirely destroyed. This put an end to all our business at present, as we did not know what would be the result of this. The joiners packed up their tools and left them and went home. As I was at this time transporting the United States Mail from Conway to Littleton twice in each week, and it being impossible to go with a horse, we carried it regularly on our backs without losing more than one single trip, to the satisfaction of our friends and employer. The directors of the turnpike came and looked over the road again, and finding it would take a large sum to repair it and make it passable for the winter, they refused, saying that the corporation was not able then to do it but must have help from some other quarter and they knew no other way for the Crawfords than that they must remain shut up by themselves, as they could not then make another road there. This did not exactly correspond with my feelings, to be entirely shut up without any communication with our southern neighbors, and not have the privilege of getting provisions and other necessary things for my family. I concluded I would try my own luck and see what I could effect myself. I set out in good earnest, took a piece of paper and a man of judgment with me, and went down through the whole length of the road and made an estimate of what I thought it would cost to repair it again. I consulted with my father upon the matter, to

know what was best to be done, then took my estimate and
went down to Portland and saw where the principal proprietors of the road lived. On my way there I called on one
of the directors and took from him a letter directed to one
of the principal proprietors and owners, to this purport,
that the Crawfords were doing a little on the road but
could not effect much, and we as a corporation have concluded we cannot do anything at present on the road, but
must let it remain in the same condition for the winter.
[Without repairs the road must inevitably be growing
worse, so that the expense in the spring must be much
greater than at this time.] After having this letter read, and
showing him what I thought it would cost to make it again,
this proprietor gave me a power of attorney to act on his
shares, and others did likewise, until I had enough to rule
the meeting, which it was then my whole business to effect.
On my way home I bought two yoke of oxen, hired men,
and set them to work on the road. The first Wednesday in
October was the time for the annual meeting of the corporation of the turnpike to adjust their business. When they
had transacted their regular affairs, it was put to vote
whether there should be an assessment raised to repair the
road. There were some against me, but I had the power in
my hands[9] and I could rule them as I pleased. I then, with
the advice of my father, voted to raise an assessment on
the shares, and that, with what other assistance we had
from Vermont and the adjoining towns around, was sufficient. We divided the broken places into jobs and let them
out to different men to make, similar to the way we had
done in former times, and we had a tolerable sleigh path
again for the winter, [and the teamsters were again hurrying their produce, pork, and poultry onward to their eastern customers over this road.] I went to Danville Bank and

hired three hundred dollars to pay off the men, and for other expenses, and, after spending a sum of four hundred dollars more, I was obliged to live without this money for nearly four years, with no interest, and could not get it until it was collected from the benefit of the road. Such was my reward for persevering and making the road contrary to the opinion of the directors, yet I could not charge them with the fault, for they did not wish to have it done until Congress could assist, or some other means could be devised to help them; but it was done, and I did not feel sorry for it, although my prospects suffered; still, as it was for the benefit of the people, and I had done it for the general or public good, I did not mind it so much as I would have done had I done it from any selfish motive. But to return to my own affairs at home: a field of grain which was partly cut, and still standing in the shocks, was swept away. As the channel of the river had been made wider in the former flood, it did not bring so much timber as at the other time, yet great quantities of sand and gravel were brought on to my interval, and the bridge and fences upon it were again carried away, and thus my mountain road was again destroyed. My loss of property was then considerable, but I did not make an exact estimate of it at that time as there did not seem to be much consolation in counting up one loss upon another. My affairs looked gloomy, and I felt almost discouraged as one misfortune kept following another, and I could not tell where my troubles would end. But in those times of trouble, Lucy was always calm and unruffled whenever she thought they proceeded from the hand of God. She received things differently from myself; seldom if ever did she complain for the want of anything but to know how to bring up our children in the right way, as they then began to be numerous; she would say there was still more work for us to do.

This fall a large number of men were at work on the road down through the Notch, and among them was a young man [from the adjoining town of Jefferson] who was subject to a kind of fits, which would take him suddenly, and sometimes when he was not aware of it. These fits did not hinder him from laboring, though in some measure they affected his mind, and so much so that they always looked after him and generally kept with or near him in order that no accident should befall him. At one time he had one of these turns after working hard through the day and at night he was tired; in the evening he showed some signs of wildness, which had been noticed by some of his companions. His father was then with him, but the young man did not wish to sleep with his father that night but slept with another man. Sometime in the night, as it appears, he was thirsty and wanted some drink; he got up and came downstairs unnoticed by the rest of the company, went out of doors, and it seemed that he lay down to drink out of a small stream of water which then crossed the road near the house, and while in the act of drinking he was taken with a fit, as it was supposed from every appearance, for in the morning when the men awoke and came down and went out of doors, they found him, lying dead and stiff, with his face in the water. How long he had lain there they could not tell. He was taken up and conveyed into the house, where a rough coffin was prepared for him. My brother Thomas being there, came to my house and got a horse and wagon, and he was carried home, followed by his father, to Jefferson, the place of his nativity, to his friends and connections, there to be interred. Here again we had an evidence of the uncertainty of life, and the importance of being prepared to meet death, let it come in whatever shape it may. This was a great grief to his friends, for they were in rather low circumstances and depended upon him for his labor to help them support an aged mother who had been blind for twenty years. She was the first female settler in Jefferson, and I think her blindness was caused by a shock from lightning which had affected her eyes, and they could not restore her sight, although some skilful physicians had tried. She lived to be almost one hundred years old.

I went to Portland and bought furniture for my new establishment and supplied it with provisions, and, January, 1829, my brother Thomas [having just] married and moved in and took charge of my new stand [at the top of the Notch.] It being a new thing, and so convenient and accommodating, he had a great share of the winter company. It was thought that this would make a great place of resort for those who would decline the more arduous undertaking of ascending Mount Washington, for just behind the house was the path which we first made to ascend the hills, and a good way might be found, one that could be made fit to ride in on horseback, by taking a zigzag course from one side of the hill to the other, which would only make the distance a little further but would make the ascent much easier; and then the eye of the curious might be almost satisfied with the sublime, magnificent, and delightful prospect from Mount Pleasant, which is not much inferior, in the opinion of some, to that from Mount Washington.

This winter I had given up the transporting of the mail, and I had no great business on hand beside my necessary employment at home. The 4th of May, Grandmother departed this life in the eighty-fourth year of her age, after struggling through several cold winters. Being afflicted with a cough, and worn out with a decline similar to that of consumption, for the cold weather affected her very much, nature at length gave way, and she could withstand it no longer. Our good neighbors and friends assembled and paid their last respects to her remains, and she was interred by the side of her husband on a piece of ground which was selected by them not far from where they had lived and slept many years of their lives together. Here their bodies will remain until called up at the last day. I have placed some suitable monuments at their graves, which can be plainly seen by their friends, and their inscriptions can be read by all who would like to see and read them.

> Their names and years, spelt by their lettered Muse,
>   The place of fame and elegy supply;
> And many a holy text around she strews,
>   That teach the rustic moralist to die.

In the spring, I gave up the idea, at present, of my carriage road to the mountain, and thought it would answer for a while to make a bridle path to the foot of it. I accordingly went to work and made a path sufficient for a horse to travel in seven miles, and I have sometimes gone further than this but not often. On arriving at the place, we would alight from our horses and take off our saddles, lay them away, tie the horses to a tree, and thus compel them to remain there until our return, without food generally, with the exception of one whose age and fidelity commanded more attention than the rest, and which at the advanced age of thirty had the spirit of a colt and would carry a visitor safely and in good style. For him I used to carry, or cause to be carried, a sack of oats as often as possible; yet this was not exactly the right way of treating the dumb beasts, to ride them on the run early in the morning the distance of seven miles, and then, in a state of perspiration, give them grain immediately, but there was no alternative. It had to be done in this way or not at all, and thus we drilled our horses from day to day, and frequently they have gone on the same route six days in a week. It was wearing to the flesh and trying to the spirits to stand all day tied to a tree and then run home again as fast as possible at night. The only time they had to eat was a few hours designed for rest, but in this way we traveled the rest of the time while I staid at the mountains, but not without remorse of conscience on my part, as our treatment of the dumb beasts was rather inhuman. But I was not able to remedy it, although I often promised so to do, by carrying in the winter on the snow a quantity of hay for them to eat when we were gone.

This summer there came some botanists from Boston for the purpose of making a collection of plants for themselves, and to collect an assortment to send to Europe, and to get some live ones to send to New York to a friend, to be placed in a botanical garden. I went with them and two other men beside, to assist them in carrying blankets and buffalo skins to make them comfortable during the night, and also other things needful for such an expedition of three days. We traveled over and around the hill; and I and one of them went down into a great gulf,[10] and here we found plenty of snow. One place I think was worthy of notice, where two ledges of perpendicular rocks stood within six or eight yards of each other, and the snow had drifted over on top of these ledges and covered them both, making a complete roof. The sun had softened this snow by day, but at night it would freeze; this had been done so many times in succession that it had formed a crust which was almost impenetrable; and I could not safely walk upon it, because it was glassy and slippery, and I could not make a dent upon it with the heel of my boot; and underneath this the ground was filled with water, and warm springs seemed to be there, which had caused the snow to melt away from under. Such was the size of this empty space that a coach with six horses attached might have been driven into it. I do not know how far this cavern extended, as I did not go far into it, for the water was fast dropping from the roof, but it appeared to be of considerable length. It was a very hot day, and not far from this place, the little delicate mountain flowers were in bloom, and here we procured as many as we chose. There seemed to be a contrast—snow in great quantities and flowers just by—which wonderfully displays the presence and power of an all-seeing and overruling God, who takes care of these little plants and causes them to put forth in due season.

As we were going up the mountain about three miles from home, where blueberries grew in abundance, we found roads in different places in the woods which were daily traveled by bears. William Howe, a brother of Lucy, being then with us, we concluded we would take a few of them if they would please to let us. We went to work in the woods and made several log traps such as are called by hunters dead-falls, as they were built in such a manner that when a bear came to one of them and wanted the bait, he would have to go in such a way that while he took hold of it, the trap would fall and generally kill him immediately.[11]

I had two steel traps, which I set also at one time. When I was gone from home, William went and found a steel trap gone; he returned home, and taking another man with him, pursued the remainder of the day, but overtook nothing. Early the next morning they again set out, and, following, found where the animal with the trap had lain the preceding night; they chased him all day but could not overtake him, and, returning homeward, came into one path some distance above where we had set these traps, and when passing them, in the dark, they heard a great noise, which seemed to them that an old bear was cuffing her cub, he cried and took on in so lamentable a manner. William was anxious to go and see what was the matter with them, but his companion would not suffer him, as he was better acquainted than William, and knew that if a cub was there confined and its mother was chastising him for his imprudence, she would be likely to show them some signs of her displeasure. They came home, and voluntarily said they would not go again after him.

Having that night returned home myself, and receiving directions from them in regard to the route, and not feeling satisfied to have such a loafer make off with my property—he all the while suffering with pain while in his thievish act—I concluded to go and look for him. Accordingly, the next morning, in company with my brother Thomas, I set out and soon found where he had lain the second night; we continued to pursue him as closely as we could trace him by the marks he made on the bushes by breaking them with the trap and laying the green brake leaves, which grow common here. I guess he began to think that Ethan, the Old Hunter, was after him in good earnest, and he was driven so hard and so closely that he probably concluded to seek out for himself a good place and then give us battle, as it appeared from the situation he was in when we overtook him. He was in a thicket, dangerous to encounter, for he was one of the long legged kind, savage in disposition, and now being covered, I thought it best to look out for him. Thomas, coming up with the gun, was desirous of demonstrating his skill in shooting him, but, as the gun had been injured by hitting it against a tree, it could not be fired easily; he however aimed at the bear's head, but to his astonishment the ball entered his forefoot, the one he had at liberty. Beginning to fear for his safety, I took the gun and reloaded it, held the lock, the affected part, firmly in my hand, and, firing, fortunately shot him through the head; he keeled over and soon died. We now released the trap from his foot, which was nearly worn off. He had managed to carry the trap and walk on three legs, on logs and over windfalls, by carrying it entirely up and clear of them. The trap when he first stepped into it was fastened with a chain and grapple; this he broke, leaving behind all but a few links, and that part which adhered to the trap did not trouble him much. We stripped him of his skin and then returned home with it and the trap, feeling justified for our humanity in releasing him from misery.

Early the same morning, William went to find out what had been the trouble the evening before, and when he came to the place, he found a small cub caught by one hind foot; it appeared true what they had heard the night before; the trap was in a measure torn to pieces, and the dirt and other stuff seemed to indicate that an old bear had been there sure enough, but did not happen to release the young one. As this cub was small, it was suffered to go entirely through excepting one hind foot, and when he took hold of the bait, the trap fell and caught his hind foot. William took hold of him and bound up his ivory, then securing his feet to keep him from scratching, brought him home alive, thinking he might be tamed and made a pet, as he seemed not much hurt, and being so young and small he supposed he might be taught as much as any other of his kind. He would also make a curiosity, as he was actually a native of the place; but either the hurt or the different position in which he traveled from what he had been accustomed to affected him, or else he intended to show proper resentment, and he died shortly after being brought home, notwithstanding he bathed him in cold water and gave him water to drink. His skin was taken off and fastened to the barn.

Shortly after this, word came about the middle of the day that there was a bear in a trap. A party from the west having just arrived, one of the gentlemen said he would go and shoot him; accordingly, we, with others, mounted horses and galloped off. On arriving at the spot, we found a good sized bear in a steel trap. The gentleman chose his distance, and this was not far, of course, as he did not apprehend any danger from the enemy now before him, for Ethan was close behind. He fired three times, resting his gun and trembling as if he were freezing (for anyone under such untried circumstances would naturally have tremor of the nerves, although naturally brave and determined), and after the third shot, I took a club or lever and finished the matter of killing him; then placing him on my horse behind, brought him home, as this was the way I was accustomed to carry game home, [and before sundown their prize was on exhibition at the Crawford House.]

Once, when going out, I found a good sized, fat, short-legged bear in a steel trap, and having a small gun, with only a partridge charge in it, I stepped up to him and put the whole contents of the gun into his face; he fell back and died immediately. It was always against my principles to keep wild animals in misery when they were in my power, or to try to sport with or torment them (further than to try their strength), because they were savage by nature; but I would relieve them from pain as soon as possible. I considered they had feelings and were not to blame for the species to which they belonged, therefore I had no right to do so; but I would treat them as well as I could. This bear weighed three hundred, and I had some difficulty in getting it on my horse. Some horses are afraid of them and sometimes get frightened by them; this was the case with the one I had, for whenever I made an attempt to put the bear on her, she would snort and jump about in such a manner I could not get him on. I then pulled off my coat, blindfolded her eyes, put the bear upon a stump, tied the horse close by, her head to a tree, and then putting my shoulder under the bear, lifted him on the saddle. I afterward rolled him back on behind, loosed the horse and then mounted the saddle myself, took off the blinders, and went on home. Perhaps we made rather an awkward appearance, but as my companion was now civil, I had no reason to complain. Still it required some care and management to keep the balance of him and look out for the horse, for she would turn her head round and see her burden, snort and stop short, and appeared to feel quite dissatisfied and uneasy with her load. This we dressed nicely, but the flesh was not of much use to my family, as there was an antipathy to it at home in consequence of stories respecting their barbarous conduct sometimes, when they get hungry and tear to pieces human flesh and devour it. No one would eat of the bear when cooked, although it smelled and tasted well. We managed to save the oil of what flesh we could not give away to our neighbors.

At another time, when going out to this now celebrated place for bears, I found a good sized yearling bear caught in a steel trap by one of his forefeet, and he appeared not to have been long there. He had fastened the grapple to a bunch of roots, and there was a chain between the grapple and the trap; here he was sitting in an humble and ashamed-looking position. I looked him over and at length concluded to contrive means to lead him home. I cut a round stick ten feet in length, sufficiently large and stout to lead him with; then taking the throat-latch from the bridle, the stirrup leather and the mail straps from the saddle, set the horse at liberty, and managed to get hold of the bear's hind feet; these I straightened and tied to a tree. I then went up to his head and secured his mouth, but not so tight but that he could lap water. While thus engaged, in spite of all my care, he put out his forepaw, the one that was at liberty, and placed it so hard against one of my legs, that I really think, had it not been for a good strong boot, he would have torn the skin, but the boot prevented him from tearing my leg; he, however, took a piece of my pantaloons with him; still I would not give up the idea of bringing him home alive. I then fastened a strap around him, before and behind, and the stick upon his neck, loosened his feet and began to try to lead him; here we had a great struggle to see which was the stronger and which should eventually be master; and he played his part so well I could do nothing with him; he would turn upon me and fight me all he possibly could. I now thought I must kill him, but as I had never been beaten by a wild animal, I was unwilling to give up now. He would come to a tree and hold on, so that I found I could not lead him. I again contrived a way to confine him, but with more difficulty than before, as his feet were entirely free, and being quick and active with them, I had hard work to get them again, but after a while I made out to. I tied his hind and forefeet together in such a manner that he could not scratch me,

were getting plenty. We felt quite easy with the thought that we were mostly free of them.

While engaged in this hunt, we discovered a beautiful little pond about two miles back of the Notch House, one of the sources of the Merrimac.[12] The appearance of this pond and its situation pleased me much, as I thought it would afford abundance of amusement for our visitors such as were fishermen. Beside this, the way in which we traveled was through romantic scenery. Leaving the main road half a mile below the Willey House and traveling in the woods half a mile, we came to a ledge of great height, impossible to climb; this we took a different course to go round. For beauty and grandeur it is nowhere surpassed by any spot to me known about these mountains.[13] This pond was well calculated for moose, as here grew the lily such as they were fond of pulling up, eating their roots. Beside, we saw signs and tracks of them recently made, but we did not happen to come in sight of any of them while hunting this fall, although one was heard; but it was dark, and he took care to make off with himself before it was light enough for him to be made a mark for the hunter.

CHAPTER X

———

Mr. Crawford's purchase of a wolf and deer.
Moose hunting. Old Abel's slide. Salting deer.
Wolves' attack upon sheep. Trout fishing.
Daniel Webster's visit. Mountain echoes. [1]

MR. CRAWFORD, always desirous to amuse his visitors, and supposing that a combination, as it were, of the nature of the forest, added to the romantic scenery, would serve to instruct as well as to gratify the eye, became anxious to get a collection of such wild animals as roamed about the hills. Although he had been very unsuccessful in retaining any alive from the large number he had captured, his ambition still caused him to seek after them.]

This winter, 1830, I had business at Colebrook. I here found a man who had accidentally come across a hollow log containing a nest full of young wolves; two of them he saved alive and tamed; these were so well domesticated that I thought it would gratify our friends and add to the novelty of our scenery to have such an animal with us. I engaged him for the next summer. He was so docile in the spring as to suffer himself to take a seat in the stage to Lancaster; then word was sent me to come for him. I went and led him home without any inconvenience, excepting when crossing the tracks of rabbits he would jump and try to follow them, and I would have to hold him fast by his chain. I brought him safely home and fastened him in the blacksmith's shop in full view of any one who chanced to pass. Our little boy tutored him and would make him howl whenever he desired. We found that when fed on animal food he was more savage than when fed upon milk. I never but once had any trouble with him, and then when going into the shop door, I stepped upon a bone which he had just buried in the dirt, and he made a violent attack upon me; I chastised him severely, and ever after he remembered it, and whenever I came near, he would appear humble, obedient, and fawning. He was as playful as any dog, but he did not like strangers quite as well; if they came near while he was eating, he would then appear cross, but he never hurt anyone.

I bought a beautiful deer, which I kept this summer, and a handsome peacock; these all amused our visitors. But there was in the wolf a kind of sly, mischievous disposition lurking within, and whenever he could get a chance, he would lie still and seem to be friendly; if a chicken would pass his way, and if he came within his reach, he would make a sudden jump and take him; and the sheep, when they passed his door, he would try hard for one of them. At one time, I tied a long rope to the end of his chain and let him into the hog yard where there was a number of swine, and an old one, who had young pigs, went at him in full rage, so much that she would not suffer him to take one of her young ones, nor give him any quarter. At another time we let him chase the calves in this way, with a rope tied at the end of his chain, and he would have succeeded in killing one of them if he had been permitted. The deer possessed a mild, peaceable, inoffensive disposition, letting anyone go near her, and would eat bread from the hands of anyone, she was so tame and gentle; but let strangers go into her pen and take her by one of her hind legs, and they could not hold her; such was her strength and dexterity that she would get away from them, do the best they could. The peacock was another favorite; he was a full grown one, and for beauty was not surpassed by any fowl whatever; he possessed a sort of pride in showing himself, and our little boy had taught him to strut, generally when he desired him. These animals were of no use to us and they were an expense, but I always liked to have such things to show to our friends and visitors, as they all seemed to be delighted in viewing them.

This summer I had no great business on hand. I spent my time mostly with my visitors at the house, and ascending the mountains whenever they decidedly requested it. But as I had been so many times up there, I was tired and worn out. I did not go when I could help it, but I always kept good and faithful guides, and every other accommodation that was in my power. The fame of this mountain scenery beginning to spread, and it becoming fashionable, many came to view these wonders of nature, and they were generally, if not always, satisfied, and considered themselves well paid for their time and trouble, and likewise they were satisfied with their fare while they staid with us. We used to tell them that whatever was lacking in substance we would try to make up in good will, and do the best we could to make them happy and their situation as pleasant as possible, and this never failed of having the desired effect of convincing them they were as much as possible at home. Among others, there came this summer four pedestrians from Boston to spend several days with us, and ascend the mountain, fish, hunt, etc. One pleasant morning three of them proposed trying the hills; they were provided with a guide and everything necessary, and set off early, while the other one remained at home with me.

As he had been up a few years before, he did not want to go again, and chose rather to try his luck in the forest.

A short time after they were gone, he took his gun and steered for the woods to a place where I directed him, and where I had in the spring put into an old rotten log some salt for deer; they found the salt and frequented it. Here he approached with great care and soon had the good fortune to see a deer, and after shooting him, cut his throat, and with the assistance of another man, returned in triumph to the house with his prize.[2] After performing the duties of a butcher, he hung him up to ripen, after which it was taken down and prepared for the table, at which he and his friends bountifully partook. During their stay with us I had a quarter of a fine fat bear sent me; it was caught in one of my traps which I had previously lent a neighbor; this they also enjoyed very much. Here they staid and spent some time, enjoying themselves in various ways, and then returned home. This feat which he performed was told when he arrived home, but was hardly credited by some of his companions. He referred them to me, and I confirmed the statement.

I went up the mountain by an express desire from a botanist, to collect plants and save them alive, for I had been there so many times with a botanist to collect plants, that I had acquired considerable knowledge of plants, and the different places where they grew. I went over the hills and came down into the gulf and then selected different species such as grow nowhere else except in the cold climate of Greenland. I carefully took them up with a quantity of earth and brought them home, placed them in a vase with some moist moss to preserve them, and then labeled the vase and sent it immediately to Boston. It was safely conveyed, and the plants were placed in a botanical garden;

how many of them survived I cannot tell, as I never heard from them afterward. The plants that were sent to New York the year before perished by the way, or rather some of the delicate ones. This was a beautiful employment, which I always engaged in with much pleasure; finding out how curiously Nature had formed them and put them in different places, according to their merits, or properties, and the state of the atmosphere in which they were destined to live.

This summer I guided several parties to the Pond. The first time I went there, we caught in a short time about seventy nice salmon trout; they differed a little from our common river trout, as they had a redder appearance, and their taste and flavor was delicious. On the bank of the Pond we struck up a fire, and after dressing a sufficient number of them, we cooked them in real hunter style. I cut a stick with three prongs to it, and put the trout on these prongs in form of a gridiron, and I broiled them over the fire; then I would cut pieces of raw pork and broil them in the same way and lay them on top of the trout, and that would give them the right relish. When cooked in this way, with a piece of good wheat bread, they made a good meal. I always enjoyed these and similar feasts in the woods, as in such ways I suppose our forefathers lived when they first came over and settled this country. We had no fears from the natives, as I expect they had in that time, but we could eat and drink without fear of being troubled. All the fish which remained after we had eaten, I took up and brought home. My visitors, I believe, were as well satisfied as myself in all these excursions, wild as they were; at least they would express themselves so.

This fall we again set our sable traps and caught a number of sable, but not so many as we would have done had it not been for the black cat, or fisher, who got the art of following the line and robbing the traps of bait, and would not then be satisfied but would take the sable from the trap and eat them. This we did not like so well, but it so happened that we could not help ourselves; they escaped being caught, although we tried hard to catch them, but they were so cunning or lucky we could not do it.

The wolves had been for a long time troubling us, and were actually so cunning I could not catch one of them, although I had, in various ways, tried. The nearest I came to catching them was by setting a trap in the water in a particular place where they frequently crossed the river. One of them sprung the trap, but it was cold weather, and ice had gathered upon it; it did not shut so closely but that he pulled out his foot, and lucky for him, he made his escape. One good haul I made while setting the trap here in the water. It so happened that a family of ducks were swimming along, and they being so near together, four of them were caught at the same time in one trap. This, we thought, was almost a miraculous thing, but it is true, for I took them all out myself and carried them to the house.

In December there came a number of wolves to visit my flock in the night, but the sheep retreated and went under the shed and got in among the cattle and carriages. Their enemy did not venture in there, although they went as far as the middle post of the shed, for we tracked them there in the morning; yet they satisfied their craving appetites, in a measure, by going just back of the stable and digging up the old carcasses of bears which had been thrown there a few months before; these they gnawed close to the bone. The dog, being shut up in the house, began to be uneasy and tried to get out, and, at length, I arose and let him out of doors, not knowing the cause of his uneasiness. He flew at them and they retired a few rods and then entered into an engagement with him, and I really think they would have made a finish of him had I not interfered and driven them away. This was by a bright moonshine, and the dog, after being first liberated from them, ran toward me, and the wolves followed closely behind him until they came near me. As I had no weapon to fight them with, being in my night dress, I observed to them that they had better make off with themselves or I would prepare for them, and that pretty soon. They then turned about and marched away, but not without giving us some of their lonesome music. There were four of them. I counted their tracks as they made them along in a light snow; and it was just day-light. As my sheep had been on the place for a long time and had taken a notion to ramble in the woods, they were troublesome to us, as we had to look them up every night, for fear of their being caught. I was determined to sell them and get rid of our trouble, which I did the second fall after this.

This winter (1831) there came some favorite hunters to go with me and search for moose, as we knew there were moose somewhere about the mountain, for two had been seen to cross the road a few months before, half a mile below my house. Everything being put in readiness, we with our dogs and snow-shoes set off. We first steered to the before mentioned Pond. We traveled all day but we found no moose, and at night we went down to my father's, [a distance of nearly thirteen miles from home;] there we staid that night, and some of our party being wearied, remained the next day and amused themselves by cutting pasteboard mininoes, while father, Mr. Davis, and myself went out in search of moose. We traveled another day, but with no better success than the former. We went up so

high and so far into the woods as to get beyond the living
animals such as we were then in pursuit of, as we could
not see a track or a sign of one, and had actually got upon
a hill from which it was difficult to get down. We struck
upon a brook which had a smooth surface, being then
frozen over, and Father, sitting down upon the heels of his
snowshoes, commenced sliding down; he had got under
good headway when he came in contact with a tree which
stood in his way, and, to save himself, caught hold of it;
this, as he was coming with such force when he took hold
of it, gave him a complete somerset and turned him completely round the tree. We came down in a similar manner, but not without fears, as it was dangerous.[3] We made
out, however, to get in that night.

The next day, as our party which we left behind had got
rested, we started for home, and on our way took some
fine deer. These we felt justified in taking, as it is said that
wolves follow when deer are plenty, and these ferocious
animals had been troublesome, making great depredations
among flocks of sheep in the neighborhood by killing a
number at a time, and many more than they wanted for
present use; but in my flock they had been more favorable,
although at one time they killed and wounded seven; however, they generally took no more than they wanted at a
time. They select the finest and fattest, and on him perform a curious act in butchering. We have found, after
they have visited the flocks, a skin perfectly whole, turned
flesh side out, with no other mark upon it excepting at the
throat where there was a regular slit cut, as though it had
been cut with a knife, down as far as the forelegs; the flesh
all eaten out, and the legs taken off, down as far as the
lowest joint; the head and backbone left attached to it; the
pelt left in the field but a few rods from the house. They

would sometimes set up a howling, and a more terrific and dismal noise I never wish to hear than this, in a clear still night. Their sound would echo from one hill to another, and it would seem that the woods were filled and alive with them.

We had some trouble with the old barn that escaped the fire in 1816, as it had received some severe shocks in the times of the freshets, and had some considerable injury done to it this winter. We had fears lest the wind would blow it over and destroy or injure the cattle; however, we propped it up, and it did not fall. I went to work and bought a sufficient quantity of lumber and brought it home for a new barn. In the spring and summer I built a new one, sixty feet long and forty wide. This I set back of the shed, and I had a communication through from the shed into it, which made it convenient for all the buildings.

This summer we had a great many visitors, and among others, a member of Congress, Daniel Webster. It was in the warm weather of June, and he desired me to go with him up the mountain, which I accordingly consented to, and we went up without meeting anything worthy of note more than was common for me to find. But to him things appeared interesting, and when we arrived there, he addressed himself in this way, saying, "Mount Washington, I have come a long distance, have toiled hard to arrive at your summit, and now you seem to give me a cold reception, for which I am extremely sorry, as I shall not have time enough to view this grand prospect which now lies before me, and nothing prevents but the uncomfortable atmosphere in which you reside!" After making this and some other observations, we began our descent, and there was actually a cold storm of snow here on the hill, while below, it was tolerably clear, and the snow froze upon us, and we suffered with the cold until we came some way down and reached a warmer climate. We returned safely home, when he related his tour to his female friends, whom he had left behind to spend the day at the house. Here they stopped again over night, and the next morning he took his departure. After paying his bill, he made me a handsome present of twenty dollars.

I had bought a little piece of artillery from the company of militia in Whitefield and put it on a little mound which was called Giant's Grave, just back, or at the end, of the barn. This I had there for the benefit of the echo, for when loaded and touched off, it would make a great noise, as it stood up in the air above the level of the surface, thirty or forty feet high, and when the air was still and clear, would echo from one hill to another, and then the sound would float along down the stream until it all died away on the ear. This was really grand and delightful, and all who heard it were well pleased, and some used to call it Crawford's home-made thunder, as it resembled the sound of thunder more than anything else. It was said that this echo was similar to that on Lake George when a gun was fired there. This cannon was made frequent use of, and for no other purpose but to amuse our friends and visitors. Once it was loaded and filled so full and jammed in so hard that it burst in touching off, and that put an end to this kind of sport then. We constantly had company in the season for it, and many were in the habit of making us presents, and among them we were presented with another gun, much superior to the former, sent to us by Mr. Gale and Mr. Gibson from Boston to Portland, and brought from there by a man who had been to market with cheese. This gun would hold half a pint of powder at a time, and the first time when we loaded it, we fired it off in the road not far from the house, and it spoke so loud that it made the house jar and cracked some glass in the windows. We then removed it to the before mentioned place where the other stood, and there it remained a few years till we had some men there who were helping us get in our hay. One night it was desired to have it fired off, and one of them loaded it with more than a proper charge and then put in gravel and drove it in hard, as he thought he would give us an explosion such as we never heard before; then with his match he touched it off, and it burst and flew all in pieces. I then sent to Portland and bought another to make up this loss, and that I left with some other interesting things at the White Hills. Some seasons we have burnt three kegs of powder in that gun.

[In 1832,] company coming from all quarters, we now suffered for the want of house room, and many times our visitors were so numerous that, for the want of beds and lodging rooms, Lucy would have to take the feather beds from the bedsteads and make them up on the floor, and then the straw beds would answer for the bedsteads. In this way we could accommodate two, and sometimes four, and frequently she would give up her own bed and lie down herself upon the floor, as she was always willing to suffer herself if she could only make her friends comfortable. But this, beside being unpleasant all round, was wearing upon the constitution too much, after toiling hard all day, to be deprived of a bed at night to sleep upon. But such are the feelings which many are subject to if they possess obliging dispositions, and more especially when they are used to misfortunes, as we had been, that nothing seems too much for our friends. As it seemed that it was not intended for us to have enough to buy such things in abundance as most of our visitors were doubtless accustomed to at home, therefore it became needful to do every act of kindness in our power. I was again advised by my friends to build an addition, which I knew was necessary, but which my circumstances, I well knew, would not admit of. I had been in debt ever since I came here to live, but I had never suffered any inconvenience by it, and I had never been called upon in such a manner as to make me any cost, with two exceptions; and after considering and reconsidering, I found I could have fifteen hundred dollars from the savings bank in Concord by paying the interest annually for a number of years, if I gave them good sureties, and having concluded to build, I mortgaged my farm and obtained the sureties required.

The roads were again good, and I expected if they remained so there would be more company every year; and as the situation of my house was such that it had a commanding view of all the mountain scenery around, and this was actually, as I thought, the only proper place for all those who desired to visit this romantic spot, although another establishment had been erected three-quarters of a mile below my house for the same purpose, which for its size and construction was well enough, yet there was but a limited prospect of the mountains there, for Mount Deception stands between that and Mount Washington, therefore all who desired to see it had to come to my house and view it from there. All who acted upon principles of honor and justice preferred this place to any other, those who lived here having beaten the bush and suffered every hardship and privation, which such a lonely place is subject to when new. I had done everything to open and facilitate a way to the mountains, and make it as good and convenient as I possibly could, therefore, in consideration of all these circumstances, I expected public patronage;

Rosebrook Place

Ethan Allen Crawford carrying a bear

and I always had a goodly share, particularly of distinguished men, and always will be likely to, I thought, at my house, if kept in good style, without having all the affluence of a city hotel, as that will not be expected so far in the woods remote from market; but always having such things as are suitable for such a place, served up in a proper manner, neat and clean, so as never to fail to satisfy persons of judgment.

It is said to be a Yankee custom that when a man is thought to be doing well there is always someone who wishes to dip into the same business, as other men think they can do better, especially if they suppose they can indulge themselves by living easily, and, by fair promises never to be fulfilled, make others work without pay for their labor; so with a man from Jefferson, in our opinion, and we have a right to our opinion and to publish it, with proper motives, for the public good. He came in the fall of 1831 and bargained for a place three-quarters of a mile below mine. I had been acquainted with him years previously and thought him friendly, as most other people are, and, also, that he was, as we were, friendly to the inhabitants around, when, one day, happening to be down where this man was, for he had come to look over the premises (which he has since left, and which, perhaps, "shall know him" now "no more forever") and make a bargain for the same, I said to him, "William, what are you here for, and where are you going?" This, by some, might possibly be thought impertinent, but it was a friendly way we had of calling one another by the given name. He answered he was going to Bethlehem to see some men there. I soon left, and this man went no further than to Mr. Rosebrook's, six miles, to the man who owned the place, and bought it of him, and, in January, was to take possession.

This clandestine management was a mystery to me, for we were pleased to have a neighbor near, and no disadvantage had arisen by the settlement, nor never would have, had this man only taken the right course. We might have been a great help to each other, as had been the case with others who lived there before him; but, instead of this, he took a different way to manage. He, in the summer, made use of my mountain road, where I had spent considerable money and which I had labored hard to make for visitors and my own benefit, and thought as much my property as any other part of my own farm, as it was made entirely at my own expense through my own land. To prevent encroachment on his part, I was compelled to make a fence and to put up a quit against him; and finding he could not have this privilege by stealth, he sent a hired man to have Richard Eastman, Esq., come down to his house, for he was there at our house, wishing him to intercede for him and see if I would not then compromise with him and let him have the privilege of my road. The Esquire told him it was then too late for this; he should have come to me himself before he had attempted to intrude upon my rights, and then there would have been no trouble in procuring this or any other favor, and we could have lived like men and have been an advantage to each other; but, instead of this, he tried to live on me and the effects of my hard labor. After this he made a path on the back of Mount Deception, and then came into my road, advertising he had made a new road, shortening the distance to the mountain. This I did not contradict in print, and thus the public was imposed upon, and I was robbed of what was actually my own property in this insinuating way.

When I first came to live here, there was a mail once a week from Maine up through the Notch to Lancaster and

Vermont, and it continued so for some time after. As the inhabitants increased, there was another mail route established from Littleton to my house, intersecting the one running through the Notch, and it was necessary for the postmaster to open it, divide it, and send packages to the directed places. I was properly appointed to transact this business, and then it run twice each week but now three times, each way, once in each working day, throughout the week, all the year. My neighbor, having a desire to take this situation of postmaster, got a petition draughted and had a false affidavit sworn to for the sake of wresting the office from me; this petition he carried about himself to the industrious inhabitants, who had not time to read it, as they said, and were not aware of what they were doing when they signed it, supposing that they were to have an office in their own town, and not disturbing mine. He succeeded in obtaining names of eighteen citizens and three selectmen, as stated from Washington, and this was another misrepresentation, as this was a new place and the town had not been organized; therefore they had no selectmen or any other officers excepting some men authorized to receive public money for schools, and that was all they had the power to do. This is a copy of the letter from headquarters.

POST OFFICE DEPARTMENT,
Office of Appts. and Inst.
AUGUST 24, 1832.

ETHAN A. CRAWFORD, ESQ.

Sir: It is presented to this Department, in an affidavit, that you have, at divers times, detained letters and papers which were directed to Phineas Rosebrook. The Postmaster General requires your answer to the charge. It is also represented by eighteen citizens and three Selectmen of Carroll, that the present location of your post-office is very inconvenient, and that the people who depend on it would be much better accommodated by its removal to the house of William Denison. The Postmaster General wishes to know if you have any objections to the proposed change of site.

I am, sir, respectfully,

Your obedient servant,

S. R. HUBBARD.

This made me some trouble, as I was under the necessity of vindicating my own character in the charge laid against me. I went to Mr. Rosebrook, myself, and he could not say as it had been stated, but only to gratify the man, who was an office seeker, had he spoken as he did; and most of those who signed the petition said they were willing to sign one against it if I wished them, but that I could do without assistance from them by my answering the letter referred to. However, he did not obtain his object; the post-office was not moved.[4]

After getting through with my summer and fall company, in the winter of 1832, as I had made up my mind to build, we had a great deal to do. As we had our glass and nails, our paints and oils, and other necessary things, to buy and bring home, we did not get ready to draw lumber until March. We then went at it with two teams, myself with one and my little boy with another, and this kept us in employment nearly two months, as it required a great quantity of lumber, such as boards, shingles, clapboards, etc., from this same before mentioned distance of thirteen miles. In the spring, I hired men and went into the woods and prepared timber for a house, and in May we raised it. It was sixty feet long and forty feet wide, two stories, with the addition of a piazza on one side, sixty feet long, two stories, and this fronts Mount Washington, east; north end, Mount Deception; south end, the beautiful green hill where deer live in the summer, since named Liberty Moun-

tain, and whence they have frequently come down into the
interval and there played and gamboled about in full view,
and many times have gratified our visitors by staying some
time in this way, and then galloping off into the woods.
Again I kept salt in an old log at the end of the meadow,
which induced them to come down there. I desired my
men never to frighten them or injure them, choosing
rather that they should come this way, than to kill them.
In the fall, this hill, like the surrounding mountains, is
richly ornamented with various colors, which, if imitated
by a painter, would make, as it would at any time, a handsome picture. And there is a one story piazza, fifty feet
long, to accommodate the traveler, as he could drive up by
the side of it and step into it right out of the carriage. I
hired six joiners, who went industriously to work, and before the last of July they had their work done, and the
painting outside was finished, so that it was ready for company, excepting plastering, which we postponed for another year.

This new addition gave us a great deal of room, which
required considerable furniture to make comfortable, without extravagance; and I was under the necessity of buying
all this, and it only involved me more and more in debt;
but still I hoped to see better times, although I did not
know when, for I was continually going from one expense
to another. Still I had paid away my money as fast as I had
received it and, I thought, to good advantage. There was,
I may say, another great expense which still hung upon
my shoulders, from which I did not know how to extricate
myself. I was obliged to keep a number of horses, for no
other purpose than to accommodate my friends a few
months in the summer, for them to ride upon the mountain; these I had to keep most of the year, on hay and

grain when used, and they were of little use beside this, the rest of the year. Then I had the most of my help to hire, which took away my coppers, as I always made it a practice to pay my hired help, if I did not pay other debts, for I always considered the laborer worthy of his hire, and all those who depend upon their own daily labor for a living ought not to be cheated, neither ought their work to be trifled with, while they who trade and get their living by speculation deserve also to be punctually paid their due, although they do not always have so great immediate necessity; but were there generally greater punctuality, there would be less failures. I have often heard it said that

> He who by the farm would thrive,
> Must either hold the plough or drive,

and sometimes I thought I did both; but it seemed I did not get ahead very fast, though I made the best I could of it, laboring myself all the time. I seldom lost a meal of victuals or a day in consequence of sickness, and I had no other infirmities, excepting at times the rheumatism which I think was caused by working in the water when living in the state of New York, and a tumor which I then thought was the piles and treated in a manner for the piles; but this was a painful thing to me. Many times I suffered greatly from the complaint without saying anything about it, and I kept it to myself for a long time. This, I suppose, was caused by going through so many heats and colds in some of the many and severe hardships which I had encountered while trying to do all I could for the public, and I sometimes went beyond my strength, and had I not more than a common constitution, I could not have stood it so long as I did. This summer we again had many visitors, and among them came a gentleman from Georgia for his health. He had fallen in company with a party which, after making their visit, took their leave of him and us and returned, while he staid some weeks. As his health was poor, he did not care much about the society of strangers, choosing rather to spend his time in the circle of our family, while he amused us, giving descriptions of his country and the manners there, which interested us very much. Sometimes he would play some tunes upon a violin which belonged to the house, and after leaving, before he arrived at home, he wrote to us, informing us his health was improved by our mountain air.

This winter, 1833, I bought a sufficient quantity of lime and brought it from Portland and Littleton to plaster my house, also paper to paper it; likewise in the spring, the mason came and plastered it, and then we papered it. We had some other troubles with our neighbor, by his encroaching on our property, beside what I have mentioned, which I will not relate. Some may say I did not like to have a man settle down near me; this, if so considered, was not so. I might have had the place where he lived, twice. The first man that bought the land, as he thought, put up buildings, but it happened that he did not buy the lot which he had built upon; this circumstance I was aware of, and I might have gone to the right owner and bought myself; but I had no disposition for an act like this. He afterward went and bought, which I was perfectly willing he should do; and, after a while, finding that he should not be able to finish his buildings and pay for the land, he came, like a man, and offered it to me, first, and wished me to buy it. This, also, I was advised to do, by my father, and he offered to assist me if I bought it; but I told him that I did not want it; furthermore, I was willing to have another establishment so that the public would not be compelled to put up with a Crawford because there could be no other place; and, if I could not do so well as to merit public patronage, I ought not to have it. One other reason induced me to have the place settled; the more inhabitants and the better the accommodations at the mountains, the more people would be likely to resort here, as they would be sure of being made more comfortable, and would not be crowded; and, moreover, they could have a choice. Sometimes we were full, also, and desired some to go to our neighbor's, and they answered, if we had but a spare peg in the house, why they could hang on that, one night, and refused thus to be turned away; so we would do the best we could for them, and make them comfortable, if possible.

This summer we had more company than usual, which kept us busy all the time from June until the last of September, and not one night were we without guests. In July, the 31st, we had seventy-five to lodge, beside our own family. Early the next morning a goodly number of the gentlemen mounted horses and set off for the mountains, in good spirits, while the remainder, many of them, staid and spent the day at the house with us. They all anticipated, the ensuing evening, a social and merry time, as they intended to have an innocent dance after the music of a violin, which was to be used by a celebrated player, as they had done the evening before; but alas! how soon may the expectation of pleasure, in this world, be cut off! They all reached the summit in good season, and, partaking of the fare carried for them by the guide, and making such remarks as they thought proper, they, at one o'clock, began to descend. One of the party being a sea-captain, said he would be the first down to see the ladies, and instantly set forward. The guide called out to him and told him he was going wrong, but he, either not hearing him or else thinking he might steer his way here on this mountain as well as on the water, went on, and they soon lost sight of him. The rest of the party kept together until they reached the horses, but saw nothing of the captain; here they found his horse and the rest of the horses and knew from this circumstance that he had got out of the way. They then came home as fast as possible and related this to his brother, sisters, and friends, who were waiting his return; they were alarmed and felt anxious for his safety.

I was called upon and consulted to know how we were to manage to find him. We then agreed that a fire should be made on or near the stream which crosses the path coming down the mountain, in case he should strike upon this stream in his wanderings and follow it down till he came to this fire; then there should be someone there to assist him home, while I should go on the mountain and search for him. We accordingly set out; his brother was to take care and manage the fire and then leave someone to blow the horn and be on the look out for the captain. I ascended the mountain, went up Jacob's Ladder, and out through the woods, that night, and called out to him a number of times, but no answer could I receive; thus I wandered about, calling to him until it grew so dark I could see no longer. I then made my way down to a temporary camp, which we had to accommodate us when at work on the road, and here I staid the remainder of the night. Early the next morning while it was yet dark, I arose and pursued after him with renewed vigor. I went again on the mountain, and again called out to him, in different places, but all in vain; no answer could I get, and I found one might as well look for a needle in a hay mow as to find a man here on the mountain, unless he had accidentally slipped and put out a joint, or broken a bone, so that he could not walk. I feared that this was the case with him, and when worn out with fatigue and hunger, began to call loudly, but I came home without finding a single trace of him. This was sorrowful news to his friends and relatives, but there was still a hope that he might find himself safe on the other side of the hills, which was actually the case. Here we will make use of his own language, as he wrote it in the album after his return.

AUGUST 1, 1833.[5]   The inclination I felt to reach a warm climate induced me to leave the party with whom I had ascended Mount Washington yesterday. After half an hour's rapid walk I found myself alone, and a little time convinced me that attempting to find them was fruitless. I then found my way to the bed of a stream, a branch of the Saco, and followed its winding for twelve miles, through briers and over rocks, from one till seven o'clock p.m., and when the approaching darkness warned me of the necessity of a bed, I discovered an object more pleasing than all the wonderful scenery that had served (though in a slight degree) to while away my six hours incessant labor. 'Twas a log bridge crossing the stream in which I was wading. Following the road with renewed vigor, I arrived in an hour at Mr. Hanson's, when a bowl of milk and a good bed left me nothing to regret but the probability of uneasiness in the minds of my friends here.

This morning I left Mr. Hanson's at five o'clock, walked seven miles to Mr. Wentworth's in Jackson, rode three miles bareback to Mr. Chisley's, who took me in his wagon seven or eight miles to Gould's, in Bartlett, whence I made the best of my way to this comfortable, temporary home, having been absent over thirty hours.

JNO. S. PAINE.

P.S. So the mountains brought forth a mouse.   J.S.P.

"GO IT YOU CRIPPLES."

Kennebunkport party obliged to leave here this day in anxious uncertainty for the fate of our cousin and friend, Lieut. J. S. Paine.

C. A. L. AND PARTY.

With hearts light and gay,
On a fine summer day,
We arrived at far fam'd Ethan's place;
When the sun shone so bright,
And all filled with delight,
We welcomed with joy each known face.

Then we wanted to go
To the mountains of snow,
And look on that scene so sublime;
But our friends said "nay,"
'Twas a dangerous way,
And the rocks we should ne'er try to climb.

So we waited to hear
What our friend Paine would bear,
From the weather, the road and the sight,
But we waited in vain,
For alas! he ne'er came,
And dreary and dull was the night.

May he come in his glory
To finish my story,
And tell of his victories won;
Then with sun beaming bright,
And hearts bounding light,
We'll farewell to MOUNT WASHINGTON.

This poetic effusion was written by the accomplished
Mrs. C. A. Lord, of Kennebunkport, as saith the album.

It is necessary for all who ascend the mountain, especially for the first time, to be governed by the guide, as the
distance of more than a mile is over rocks without any surface to make any path or track, and unless the stranger
takes particular notice of the way in which he goes up, he
may, like the captain, get mistaken and take a wrong
course. Several years ago, when it was the custom to go
out and camp at the foot of the mountain, then, early in
the morning, ascend the hill, a young Vermonter with

some others came and went there and staid, and early in the morning set out to climb the hills. There came on a thick mist of rain after they had started, but he being persevering determined to go on, and for fear he should lose his way when he should come back, laid up piles of stones, as monuments or guides, at proper distances from each other, so that travelers should not get mistaken or lost, which remain in honor of him at this day and have been of use to many, who were like himself, determined to pursue after they had undertaken it. He, however, returned to the camp after reaching the summit, sent the guide home for new supplies of provisions, and there they remained until they had a clear day. Such was the spirit of a Vermonter.

I do not recollect anything more, particularly interesting, that took place this summer, worth mentioning, but suffice it to say, we had plenty of company until quite late in the fall, and some after the snow had got so deep that they could not reach the top of the hill.

1834.   Now as I was satisfied, for the present, with building, I had not much business on hand excepting that of buying and bringing home supplies for the season. I spent my time principally with my family. Home, with me, was always delightful, after spending the day in different exercises and getting weary. To be able to sit down and have half a dozen little ones come and rest themselves upon me, all of them having good reason and proper shapes, which was a great satisfaction to me, was considered a blessing. In April, one week after the birth of our ninth child, Lucy took cold,[6] and as she had been accustomed to administer physic to her family when unwell, she now thought she would prescribe for herself. She then ordered a dose of hygean pills to be handed her, and took a large portion of them; but as these had not the desired effect, she took another, which, as her physician told her afterward, was the means of saving her life at that time, but did not restore her to health. She remained sick and feeble, with a slow fever. I then sent eighteen miles for a physician who came and gave her such things as he thought proper, but did not remove the cause. We sent and he came again; but no better did she get. Her case was now a desperate one. The child, for want of proper nourishment such as is natural for children, grew very worried and fretful; this served to add another trouble to Lucy, as she had always been healthy and could satisfy her infants by nursing them, but, at this time, it only seemed to injure and not satisfy it; and as she had the feelings of a mother, she said she did not know how to bear with its cries. A friend, a gentleman from Portsmouth, calling at my house at this time, when going on business to Jefferson, saw the situation of Lucy, and she having a brother living there, whose wife had just lost an infant, they sent me word by the gentleman upon his return from Jefferson that if I would bring the child to them, they would take care of it. This information I received late at night, and when communicating it to Lucy, she seemed rejoiced to think the child was provided for. I brought up several objections to her against parting with it; told her that if they nursed it, most likely their affections would be so great for it they would not be willing to give it up; all these things she could do away with if she could but know it comfortably taken care of. Her mind being fixed, suitable preparations were made for its removal. My courage began to fail, and I asked Lucy if we had not better wait and bring her brother's wife over here? She said, no, as it would be a long time before she would be able to come, and she could not bear the sufferings of the babe any longer. It was then wrapped up, and after it had received the parting kiss from its mother, which was imprinted with a tear, for which she received a smile in return, for the child was then six weeks old, I took it in my arms on horseback and carried it sixteen miles, without a murmur or a cry from the child, by stopping twice on the way and feeding it out of a bottle which I carried in my pocket, which had been previously prepared for it. The child was welcomed by its new mother, and after receiving plenty of nourishment, it became satisfied. I returned home and related my tour and good success in the conveyance of the babe, and the satisfaction it appeared to take in a new mother's bosom. This, Lucy said, was an act of Providence, for which she hoped to be thankful. As Lucy got no better, I was advised to send thirty miles for another physician, who succeeded no better than the former one in removing the cause of her complaint. I likewise had the advice of several old and experienced ones, but all to no purpose; she remained sick, weak, and in great pain most of the time. She was told by her friends it was not likely she would ever recover, or arise from that bed of sickness; this did not seem to affect her in the least. She kept up good courage, as she was desirous of getting well, knowing that she had a large family of her own, beside Uncle William to take care of, and much there is depending on a mother in bringing up her children. These things she took into consideration with a firm belief that God would, in his wise providence, see fit to send some means to help her; and after lying in this helpless situation from April until July, her desires were answered. Doctor Warren, with his family, from Boston, came to spend a few days with us; and his good lady, having been here before and learning that Lucy was sick, came immediately into the room and seeing how she was, said she would go for

the doctor. He came in and examined her, but did not prescribe anything for her at that time. He came the third
time to see her and then wrote a prescription for her,
which as soon as it was obtained, helped her, and in a few
weeks she was able to be about with her family. All this did
the doctor without receiving a single farthing, for he would
not accept of compensation for his trouble or advice, for
which we are still indebted to him.

Likewise we are under many obligations to a number of
people of Boston, for their kindness, their attention, and
presents during the summer.

My affairs at that time began to look gloomy; sickness
had ever been a stranger at our house, now it became an
associate there. Our next youngest child was dangerously
ill of the bowel complaint, and company began to shun my
house, which was on account of the influence of stage
drivers, as our neighbor, having made some addition to
his establishment, offered to keep their horses on hay, free
from any expense to them, if they would influence the
company and bring the passengers to his house. Of this I
was verbally informed by them, but as I was then keeping
them at a very low rate, I did not know how to keep them
for nothing, and of course they removed their quarters. I
had done much for them in making the place fashionable,
which caused them to have passengers, who paid them
handsomely for riding in their stages. This I thought
would be enough to insure their patronage without an explanation to them. The owner of the line had been pro-
moted to some public stations, which should have in-
sured better principles within his mind than to have let
him practice upon such a low, narrow, contracted one,
just for the sake of saving a trifle, and try to injure me in
this way at a time when I was in trouble. How much this

added to their interest, or to the credit of the stage and its owner, I am not able to say; one thing I know, it was an injury to me, as I depended upon my customers for money to pay for extra expenses which I had incurred by building and making things good and comfortable for their convenience. Some people are so avaricious that they must have their own way even if it hurts the honest and industrious ones ever so much, as was the case, I think, with the one just mentioned. I, however, made the best I could of it, hired money to pay some debts, and other creditors I pacified with promising them they should have their pay as soon as possible. In the fall, as I was returning from Lancaster on horseback, in the forenoon I called at a six mile neighbor's and there borrowed a fan for the purpose of clearing up some grain, and when coming down what is called Cherry Mountain, the horse made a misstep which brought him on his knees; being encumbered with the fan, I had not the means of saving myself, and I was brought suddenly across the pommel of the saddle; this struck an affected part of my body and hurt me very much. The horse recovered himself, and I regained my seat upon the saddle. I went home that afternoon and assisted in fanning up twenty bushels of wheat. Standing in the air, so that the air might carry away the dust which arose from it, and perspiring, I took cold, which settled where I was most liable, and that night my bowels began to swell and continued to for three days, and a man in greater distress than I was, I would think never need be. I neither ate more than three crackers nor slept the whole time. I had a high fever which caused me to be thirsty. I drank freely of cold water, which only increased my pain. I took physic, one portion after another, without any effect. I grew worse and worse until at length I told Lucy I must die; I had no desire to live in so much pain. She remonstrated with me, saying I had been the means of bringing a large family into the world, which was depending upon me for support, and I ought not to indulge such thoughts but should keep good courage, and perhaps there would be a relief. I asked her when? Oh! she said she could not tell when, neither did I know how much I could bear until I had the trial put upon me. She told me to be patient and perhaps God, who had let me suffer, would in some way cause relief. Well, I said, I would try one more thing. I would take half a tea-cup full, or more, of Epsom Salts dissolved in water; this was prepared and I swallowed it. Now, said I, if this does not answer the purpose, I must bid you and the children farewell. I began to pace the room; things looked strangely, and I had such feelings as I cannot describe if I attempt it. This did not last long before I felt the salts begin to operate, and I soon found relief from them. As soon as I was able to ride, I went to Littleton to a physician and told him my case; he said I was a tough one and wondered I had lived through it, as mortification was near at hand at that time. He then gave me some medicine and advised me to be operated upon as soon as I could get a surgeon, or it might in time cost me my life. Other physicians, also, told me the same story. This I thought I could not live through; I still held the idea that I might as well die with it as to die while undergoing such an operation, for I thought it would certainly kill me.[7]

In the winter of 1835, as I had expressed some desire of selling my place and settling my affairs with the world in consequence of ill health, for I was not able to do much or go from home but little, one night in April there came a man from Bartlett to make propositions to buy my place. He was then going to Boston, and knew of a certain stage

company who would buy it, as he thought, and, in so doing, would confer a favor on me. I thanked him for his
good intentions, then went to work and bonded it to him
for six months, for ten thousand dollars; this he wished to
have kept a secret for a short time. My father, coming in
before the close of the business, wanted to know what the
man was there for; but as I had promised not to speak
about it, I did not tell him. The old gentleman said afterward, if I had told him or if he had known it, he would
have advised me better. In a short time the great cry of
speculation in land was heard on all sides, and I could
have sold it for two thousand dollars more than I had
bonded it for, but as I had never been in the habit of
making children's bargains, there should be no grunting
on my part.

Now to fill the place of the little one we had parted with
the year before (as what I had predicted proved true, for
those who had taken the child, unnamed, and nursed it so
long, claimed it as their own, having no other, and we
seemed rather compelled to give it up to them), we had
another child born in May, which gave us ten in number,
five sons and five daughters. Nine of them are still living.
While in this solitary place, so far from human assistance,
Lucy did not put her trust in an arm of flesh to save her,
but she trusted to a higher power, and was carried through
every trial, for which she had great reason to be thankful.

The man coming home from Boston, sent me word that
I might depend upon the money before the time of the
bond running out, and I made little other exertions to get
money to pay my debts with, supposing this would be the
case. As the bargain was so good, I thought there would
be no failure upon his part, and depended upon it. He
went again, and found a good company of speculators,

who had money deposited in a bank in Boston, and every arrangement being made, the papers were drawn in the evening for eleven thousand dollars, of which ten thousand was to be paid him, and he was to have a share with them of one thousand himself; the next morning when they met again to close the bargain, no papers of the evening could be found. This disaffected the company, and they would do nothing more about it, as they supposed the man thought it was going so quickly that he might have more; therefore, took no care of the papers.[8] But the man says that they were lost by the clerk who kept the office where they did their business. Which of these two was the cause of this mistake, I am unable to say, but it was a sad one for me, as I had depended so much upon it, and might have done so much better had it not been for my reliance upon this; but it seems to show the uncertainty of man and how little dependence can be placed even on those we think our friends. I always thought this man my friend, having been acquainted with him for years, but so it happened, and there was no help for it on my part. I was informed of all the particulars of this transaction by one of the company which thought of buying. I asked the man to give me the bond, which he said I might have, but I could not get it. He then told me he would try again to sell it, and still thought he could dispose of it advantageously both to himself and to me; but this was all a humbug. He still kept the bond until it died in his hands. He, however, lost nothing more than his time and trouble, with the exception of what he intended to make, as he had not paid me anything for it.

During the summer we had a goodly share of company, notwithstanding the stage drivers' influence and that of some tavern-keepers who were interested in this concerted plan of leading company to the wrong place; and many whom they did decoy came to my house and said they were misled and should not be caught again in that way; but as I was then suffering with the complaint before mentioned, I felt little ambition about the proceeding of things, at times, but let them do pretty much as they did; and at other times I felt the abuse and then tried to vindicate my own rights, but this I could not carry into effect, owing to the state of my mind, as this complaint centered in its effects mostly in my head.

After this, I strove to sell, but the fever of speculation had then begun to abate, and I could not get more offered for it than enough to pay what I was then owing, which was not as much as the buildings had cost; this I could not in conscience take, as the place was actually worth so much more. So we continued to stay longer and do the best we could.

My complaint increased, at times troubling me very much, and this winter, 1836, I was advised to send to Concord and obtain some of Dr. Morril's patent medicine, which was celebrated for effecting great cures; I was told that perhaps it might reach my case. I wrote to him, and in return received the medicine with directions. These I followed as nearly as possible, but it only made me worse, instead of better, having a tendency to heat and stimulate, which was contrary to the manner that my complaint should have been treated; yet I did not think any one was to blame in the matter. My friends being anxious that I should get well, said I must keep trying, and if one thing would not do, try another; this I did, but all to no purpose.

This winter, as deer had become plenty in the woods, many parties went in pursuit of them, and my eldest son, Harvey, possessing the same disposition as others, desired to go with them, but as his constitution was not equal to that of others, I did not consent to have him go with them.

In March, a gentleman came to my house who had been traveling some years, and his horse being weary, he concluded to stay a few days and rest him. He being a sportsman, soon contracted for a little fun with Harvey; and as I had ever been against his going into the woods with others, I then concluded to let him go.

They were prepared accordingly, and in the afternoon set out. They steered nearly south of my house and went up the green hill where deer were plenty, and having arrived there in season, built them a camp and spent the night finely, as they expressed it. Early in the morning before they had breakfasted, not being experienced hunters, as they were anxious to find what they were in pursuit of, they left their lodgings and victuals all together, and went out upon a tour of observation or discovery, intending to return and breakfast shortly. After leaving the camp, the dog went into a yard of deer and followed them, and they found there was no time to be lost and were obliged to pursue as fast as possible on snow-shoes, or they would lose both dog and deer. They soon came up with the dog, who had a deer; they cut his throat and took out his inwards and left him there. The dog pursued others in a similar manner, and they caught three of them. By this time hunger began to call loudly upon them; as they had been in a hurry, and unmindful of the course they had taken, they were so bewildered among the hills that they were not sure what course to take to make for home. They, however, struck upon a small stream, and followed it down to the Amanoosuc river, nearly three miles below my house, leaving their game behind, tired and hungry enough.

The next morning I observed to them it was not customary for hunters to leave their game in the woods to
spoil, and thought they had better go and bring theirs in,
or else we should have to take their word for what they had
done. The gentleman said he was satisfied to let his part
remain where it then was rather than go the route over
again. He had had a pleasant time and a lucky one in
hunting and found himself at home; he was then on good
footing and thought he would keep so. But as Harvey had
for so long a time been wanting to hunt, I told him he
must go and bring home his game; and after getting rested
he took a hired man and went after it. He, not being yet
satisfied, thought he would wander about and perhaps
might find a deer, one that he could catch and lead home
alive, as I had done. The south wind beginning to blow
strong, and the clouds coming on, it was dark before they
were aware of it, and they could not find the camp which
had been built but two days before, where they intended
to spend the night, and in consequence of the darkness
they were lost and could find no other shelter than a large
hemlock tree. They had barely the means of obtaining fire,
and that was all. Their axe, provisions, and everything
conducive to their comfort were at the camp, while they
were compelled to stay and draw out a long night in that
season of the year. The wind blowing violently made the
trees writhe and bend on all sides of them. The rain descended in great profusion upon them, and they had nothing to shelter them from the impending storm. But they
were fortunate in getting fire in a dry tree, which was some
satisfaction, but not much comfort to them, as all the good
this did was to burn one side while the other was shivering
with the wet and cold. The snow being deep, they had
nothing to stand upon beside their snow-shoes, and in this

perilous condition they spent a long night. They said it was the longest one they ever knew.

They suffered greatly from fear of being killed by falling trees, as they fell occasionally near them, but the same Preserver who took care of them in sunshine cared for them then, and they were permitted to behold the light of another morning with gladness, and in a few minutes they found the camp, but a little way from where they had spent such a miserable night. They then provided themselves with a comfortable breakfast, and, after resting awhile, started for home. They had the preceding day gathered some of the venison, and tried to bring it home, but the snow was so deep and soft that their snow-shoes would sink deep, and it was with difficulty they could raise them, and they were obliged to leave it there and make their best way home, where they were welcomed.[9] I think parents were never more rejoiced than we were when we saw Harvey coming across the field, as our anxiety had been so great through the night that neither of us had slept. After that I was not troubled any more with being teased by him for want of hunting. He was now satisfied.

But to return again to myself. Sometimes I would seem to be quite well, and then I did not mind my sickness so much as at other times; then there would a pain catch me in the spine of my back and run over me like a flash of lightning, even to the top of my head, and every hair would seem to move. Many times I have put my hand to the top of my head and felt the hair to know if it did not stand straight on end, as I could feel it rise, and sometimes would think it would throw off my hat. The pain from my back centered in my head, which caused me to be forgetful. They who had ever been my nearest and best friends had become my enemies, as it appeared to me, and from no other cause than my being sick and in trouble when I most needed consolation, and this caused me sometimes to be irritable, which was not exactly my natural disposition, but I knew not how to help it then. My appetite was gone, and I was attended by a cough and afflicted by raising great quantities of phlegm; my blood was reduced, and I would have extremes of heat and cold pass through my veins, one after another. Sometimes in the morning I would think I could get up and should be smart that day, but after getting up and only walking in another room, I would begin to shiver with the cold and have to go to bed again, and have my pillows warmed and placed on my back, and blankets warmed and put upon me. In this way I lived by turns until I was returning from Conway in the stage, having been down on business in company with Dr. Bemis,[10] from Boston, and some other gentlemen beside him, when I was attacked with this complaint, and had, in the stage, two spasms, which required the strength of a man to hold me. This sudden and unexpected shock was below my father's, and I did not then think I should live to get home, but I meant to go along as I could. I had the kindest assistance from the gentlemen in the stage, and arrived at home, where I soon after had another spasm. Lucy sent immediately for a physician, who arrived and took away a portion of blood, which soon relieved me. This kind and humane Dr. Bemis, who was then staying at my house, became acquainted with Dr. Rodgers, from New York, who had previously, before he started, been directed to put up with me, but was influenced by some other persons to stop with my neighbor. Dr. Bemis informed Dr. Rodgers of my situation, and he came to see me, told me unless I would consent to have an operation, I could not live long, as the consumption was near upon me; said he would go and get his instruments, while another physician who was with him should stop and make preparations for the same. This I did not consent to, neither did I refuse it. The doctor returned in a short time, and due preparations being made, went upstairs with them, when the operation was performed.

How estimable is the character of a good physician, or of any really good man! While "man's inhumanity to man makes countless thousands mourn," so the kind ministrations of man to man proves that God gives us in charge of his angels.

I then came down with them and soon found relief. I now could sit in a chair much better than for months before. The doctor came and dressed my wound several times himself and then showed another person how to manage it, and when he took his leave, I asked him how much I should pay him. He said not anything, but he expressed a desire for me to get well. For this act of kindness I am indebted to Dr. Bemis for his interceding as he did in my behalf, and Dr. Rodgers for his assistance. I am well persuaded, had it not been for them I should not now have been here a living man. Times had now become hard, and my creditors, who had waited on me, were afraid they should not get their pay, because my dissolution, as they thought, was near at hand, and in the course of the preceding summer they had come upon me like a set of armed men. I turned out all my personal property, even to the last cow, and some articles I turned out three times, I was afterward informed, but the state of my mind was such, owing to the pain in my head, I was not sensible of what I did. In the fall, before I was able to get about much, a deputy sheriff came from Lancaster for me to pay a sum of three hundred dollars which I was owing the bank and one more demand due a farmer for about forty dollars, principal, but as he had taken care not to have it reduced by interest and cost, which he had caused to be doubled, I told him I had then nothing to pay with but desired him to be patient as they were not suffering for the money, and they and every other creditor should have their honest dues if they would only show me lenity. He then left me, after obtaining a promise on my part that as soon as I was able to ride, I would go to Lancaster and see them myself, and some days after, according to promise, I went, and what do you think these men did? Why, for want thereof, took my poor and emaciated body and cast it into prison, although a brother of mine and one of Lucy's offered to give them bonds for my appearance at any time whenever they should call for me. But this did not seem to pacify them; they were determined upon other purposes; their object was money, and they refused to take them. I was put in jail, and this place was to me a complete hell upon earth, now shut up from air and the society of my beloved family.

My mind was weak, and the time hanging heavily forced me to reflect on human nature; this overcame me, and I was obliged to call for the advice of physicians and a nurse. Here I was attended with a sort of spasm similar to the former ones, and was really so unwell that one of my physicians affectionately told me he thought I should never pass the Gun hill that was near the burying-ground; that was as much as to say I should die. He then asked me if they should not send for Lucy. I told him no; it was enough for me to be there and not her. Here they kept me twenty-five days in this way. I had applied to an attorney before I went in to make arrangements for me to take the benefit of the law, in such cases made and provided, and when the time arrived they told me I could not do it without perjuring myself. I told them something should be done, for I would stay there no longer. They then concluded to take our brothers for sureties and let me go home. This added nothing to their interest, neither did it help them immediately to their pay. They were secured before. I had good signers with me on the notes, and my farm was holden, but when a man gets going downhill, it matters not what shape it is in, there are enough standing ready to give him a kick and help him down. They have since got their pay, but the tanner dares not look me in the face and say, How do you do? but passes by as soon as convenient; they will have to answer to their Judge. Lucy wrote to him in the most affectionate terms, intreating him in the name of a husband and a father to go and see me and advise some means to let me come home, and sent it by the hand of her son, who handed it to him; he read the contents and put the letter in his pocket, and never came near me till the day that I was set at liberty.

Having been for so long a time racked with pain, and having now these troubles, I did not seem to get much better of my complaint, and was advised by some friends and my family to give up my farm and retire to a more secluded spot where health might be regained. Accordingly, for that present time, I changed situations with a brother of Lucy's and moved to Guildhall, in Vermont, the place of our nativity.

Before we left we sent to those men to whom I had mortgaged my farm to come and take possession of it, which they did, and I suppose, in a lawful manner, put up an advertisement in the house to sell it on the 16th of March, 1837. It was then subject to two mortgages, Uncle William's was one and the other was theirs. The amount of theirs was to be made known at the time of sale, but as it appeared, no one came to buy, therefore they had the whole management of the affair to themselves. At this time Lucy was there, and I expressed a regret to leave the place where we had performed so much hard labor, and had done everything to make the mountain scenery fashionable, and had just got in a way to make ourselves comfortable, and to be able to make our friends feel at home. It was hard to give it all up and let it go into the hands of others. One of them made her this reply, saying, fifty years hence it will be as in old time; there would be those rise up who knew not Joseph, and it would not then be known who did all these things. They then rented it for one year, and at the expiration of that year rented it again to the same man for five hundred dollars per annum.

While we were at Guildhall, as there was a sugar lot on the farm, I thought I would make sugar that spring with the help of my little boys, and as Lucy was always anxious about me when absent, particularly then on account of my health and misfortunes, I happening one night to stay away later than usual, she thought something might have befallen me, as I had only one boy with me, so after putting her children to rest at nine o'clock, she took a lantern and steered for the woods. Never having been there before, she lost her way and was actually under the necessity of calling for help. The boy having amused himself peeling birch bark while I was engaged in boiling sap, we put some of this dry bark on the end of a pole which was long, set it on fire, and raised it up so high in the air that she saw it and then came to us and staid until we could all go home together, where we arrived at eleven o'clock.

We remained on this place ten months, where we raised barely enough to support our family. As Lucy's brother must lease our farm at the mountains, it being put into other hands, he was then wanting his own to live on, so I went down the Connecticut river one mile, and engaged a large two story dwelling-house, which was then unoccupied, for the farm had been rented to its nearest neighbor, and I obtained the use of it until April, when his lease would run out. Sometime this winter, a gentleman by the name of Jonathan Tucker, Esq., who had an execution against the farm I was then living upon, came from Saco, Maine, and the marshal of the state came also, and set off, to this Mr. Tucker, nearly fifty acres of the best part of the land, with the barn. This is the very place where our grandmother lived when she had so much trouble with the Indians. I have tilled the same ground where their little log cabin used to stand, which was near the bank of the river. Afterward, they or others built upon higher ground. When this land was set off, I asked Mr. Tucker if I might have the privilege of improving it. He told me to stay and do the best I could, and if it were redeemed he should have nothing more to do with it, and the defendant in the case had six months for redemption; if it were not redeemed, I could have a living from it. According to human nature in these days, reader, how do you think this man let us live here after the redemption ran out? I wrote him an account of our management and asked him if I might pay the lawyer who had assisted in obtaining this land. He said I might.

Thus we lived upon this beautiful farm, while we had the privilege of raising every kind of grain and vegetable, such as corn, rye, oats, peas, beans, potatoes; and we had a first rate garden, surrounded with currants, gooseberries, and plums. As the river went round this meadow in a semicircle and made a bow in some places, there was

capital fishing, where my boys could catch plenty of pick-
erel, some trout, dace, eels, etc. This made quite a market
place, as these fish make grand living when cooked with
good salt pork. Here we could send our children to school,
six and seven months in a year. One winter we furnished
the school with nine scholars, our own children, for which
we received the credit of the committee, for, as the law
was, every scholar drew a proportion of the public money,
and the more scholars there were, the longer the school
continued. We likewise had every privilege which is common in towns, such as meetings for divine worship and
good society among our own relatives and friends.

As we had always been used to labor ourselves, we instructed our children, when quite young, to be diligent in
whatever they could do; and this seemed to be a great help
to them as they could earn their own living, and being
accustomed to work at home, they were not ashamed to go
abroad. When they were not at school, those of them that
could be spared from the farm and dairy, for we had cows
and made butter and cheese, could support themselves at
home or abroad, respectably; while I could do mason
work, as I had assisted in helping plaster my own buildings and learned how to make mortar, and could, then,
spread it well, and I could earn my dollar per day when I
worked at my trade. In this and similar ways, according to
the customs of New England, we lived on this beautiful
farm by paying the taxes and keeping the buildings in repair, which we consider to be an act of benevolence from
this Mr. Tucker, and for which we will return our gratitude. There are but few men in these days who would do
so much even for a relative, without some direct compensation from him, if nothing more than a promise, for which
he never made me a request. But the fifth year a lawyer

who lived in Lancaster, by some means obtained a lease of the place, and we were obliged to give him half we raised on this piece of land belonging to Mr. Tucker. There seemed to be quite a contrast now, after living in the way just described and now obliged to go halves with this lawyer, which did not exactly suit my family, working hard as usual, when they had the whole before.

In 1843, I hired the large three story building, which was then empty, in sight of where we had lived twenty years at the mountains, and here we are at the present time in 1845.

It may be an inquiry how these things have come to be written. Lucy had been advised to keep a memorandum of things as they occurred, for there seemed to be something very extraordinary in our affairs in life, which was an inducement for her labor, in which she has taken great pleasure, in order to be able to show the public our way of trying to get a living, by dealing honestly with men and having a clear conscience as regards my management with mankind. Moreover, the men to whom I had given up my farm said they were willing for us to have it again by our refunding them whatever they had paid out, with the interest and cost, provided Lucy would publish this history, which, after being published, she could sell and it would be an assistance. As we were then retired from the cares of other people and had nothing but our own family to look after, she found time.

It is the request of some of my friends to have a genealogy of my father's family. Abel Crawford is now eighty years of age when this year, 1845, shall have passed away, and he was the first man that ever rode a horse on the top of Mount Washington.[11] He was then aged seventy-five, and is now a well, stout, athletic man, capable of doing

work and business. My mother, who was Hannah Rosebrook, is in her seventy-fourth year, enjoying tolerably
good health, after having raised a family of nine children.
Erastus, their eldest son, was born in 1791, and grew up a
large, stout, and tall man, six feet six inches high when
standing barefoot. After he was twenty-one he went into
the state of New York, where he lived and married, and
his wife had two sons, and then he died there in 1825; these
two sons of his are now nearly the same height their father
was when he was living. Ethan Allen is my name, and I am
fifty-three, with much better health than when I left the
mountains. Stephen was born in 1796, and he died when
he was fifteen years of age with the consumption. Everett
has a wife and four children, three sons and one daughter,
and lives in Jefferson, New Hampshire. Dearborn lives in
Orford, New Hampshire, and has a wife who has borne
him ten children, six daughters and four sons. Thomas J.
lives at the Notch House which I built in 1828, with his
wife and four children, all of them daughters. Hannah H.
is married to Nathaniel T. P. Davis, and they live in Hart's
Location with my parents, who have lived there fifty years;
she has two children, both daughters.[12] Abel J. has a wife
and one child, a son, and lives in Jefferson, New Hampshire. William H. Harrison still lives at home with Mr.
Davis, enjoying life at his ease, without any care or trouble
of a family, living in a "state of single blessedness." Uncle
William Rosebrook, who was spoken of in the first part of
this history, is seventy-two years of age and still lives with
us, enjoying good health. He never was married. Lucy, my
wife, has had ten children, five sons and five daughters.
Harvey Howe, not having a strong constitution, learned
the art of making wagons and has gone into the state of
Ohio. Our second son died when an infant. Lucy Laurilla,

Ellen Wile, Eluthera Porter, Ethan, Stephen, Persis Julia, Placentia Whidden, and William make out our number.

And now my friends who have a little time to spare, or whose health is impaired, come to the mountains and make us a visit. You will find us here, and there shall be no pains spared to make your time pass pleasantly during your stay with us, either in waiting on you or giving you all the information in our power, and, as of old, what we lack in substance we will endeavor to make up in good will. We gratefully return our warmest thanks for the public patronage which we formerly received while at the mountains, and we still hope by our united exertions to continue to merit it. When you get to Conway, if coming in that direction, you will find excellent treatment in a Temperance House kept by Colonel Hill, the postmaster, where you will have entered the mountain scenery, and where, in fair weather, you will see the ranges of hills, or mountains, rising one above another along the way, and when passing, reflect on the mighty works of God, and think what the labor of man, in a few years, has accomplished.

The town of Conway, situated about twenty miles south of the White Mountains, began to be settled about the year 1776 by emigrants from Concord, Durham, Lee, and the adjoining towns. The glowing accounts which the hunters gave of the extensive tracts of interval bordering on the Saco river, which runs through the same, the fertility of the soil, the exuberance of its forests, especially its sugar maples and white pines, together with its numerous wild animals and fowls, all conspired to facilitate its settlement. At the close of the Revolutionary War, in 1783, Conway had become more numerously settled than almost any other inland town of its age and size in New Hamp-

shire. Its early inhabitants, however, were obliged to endure great hardships in conveying their furniture and provisions through a wilderness of sixty miles in extent upon
pack-horses and hand-sleds.

They soon began the lumber business by floating logs
and masts down the Saco to its mouth, where they received bread stuff and other necessaries of life in exchange,
the moose and deer at the same time affording them a
tolerable supply of wild meat, and their white and rock
maple trees an abundance of excellent sugar. The rivers
and ponds were also well stored with wild geese, ducks,
and fish of various kinds. In consequence of these con-
veniences, the richness of its soil, and its healthy climate,
Conway has now become a very pleasant town, dotted
with several handsome villages, and containing about two
thousand inhabitants.

Colonel David Page, Joshua Heath, Ebenezer Burbank,
John and Josiah Doloff, were the first who moved with
their families to Conway. They came by the way of Saco,
in the state of Maine, thence up the river and across
Lovewell's Pond to the Seven Lots (so called) in Frye-
burg, which town adjoins Conway, and had commenced
settling in 1764 by Moses Ames, Esq., and six other
families.

It was at the head of this pond, which lies about two
miles east of Conway, that Captain Lovewell and his company fought their sanguinary battle with Captain Paugus
and his Indians on the 8th of May, 1725, and in which
both commanders and three fourths of their men were
slain, consisting at the commencement of thirty-four
Englishmen and eighty savages. These Indians belonged
to the Pequaket tribe, inhabiting the country from the
Notch of the White Mountains to the Great Falls on the

Saco river, about sixty miles in extent, which has borne the general name of Pequaket ever since, from that circumstance.

[Captain Lovewell left Dunstable with forty-six men under his command, principally volunteers from the towns in that vicinity. Upon his arrival at this place, nearly worn out by fatigue in traveling through so long and dense a wilderness, his men reduced to thirty-four, they came upon a portion of the Pequaket tribe. . . . It appears that the Indians were aware of the approach of the whites and endeavored by stratagem to divide Lovewell's men that they might more easily conquer them. After Paugus had struck upon the trail of his enemy, still and silent were his men ordered to move until he had learned the strength of the opposing force, when he secreted his blood-thirsty warriors among the tall grass growing upon the bog. The attack commenced about ten o'clock in the morning and was warmly contested till nearly dusk. During the early part of the fight, so great was the difference in number between combatants that the whites became fearful, after losing so many men, that the savages would surround their little band, that they beat a retreat to a ledge of rock where they could be better protected; the Indians, at last becoming convinced that the palefaces were determined to conquer or die, fled to the forest. The savages, it is supposed, lost about sixty of their number, while but fifteen of the whites found their way back to the settlements, and part of those were in so emaciated condition that it was a long time before health was restored to them. Record shows it to have been one of the bloodiest and hard-fought conflicts of the early settlements.][13]

The town of Bartlett, lying between Conway and the Notch of the White Mountains, originally consisted of several locations, granted to William Stark, Vere Royce, and others in consideration of their services as officers in the French war in Canada. Enoch Emery, Humphrey Emery, and Nathaniel Herriman began their settlement in lower Bartlett just before the commencement of the Revolutionary War, their land being given them by Captain Stark for settling. In 1777, Samuel Willey, Esq., Daniel Fox, and Paul Jills, from Lee, purchased a tract of land in upper Bartlett and commenced clearing the same. Their horses, which they had turned into an adjoining meadow to graze, became dissatisfied with their new location, together with their manner of living, and started for home. Instead of following the windings of the Saco in the path they went up, they struck off in a straight line. In crossing the first intervening mountain, it is supposed they became separated and consequently bewildered. Diligent search was made for them but all in vain.

The next spring a hunter's dog brought part of a horse's leg into the road in Conway. From a particular mark on the shoe attached to the foot, it was ascertained to have belonged to Mr. Willey's horse. On following the dog's track, about sixty rods from the road the carcass was found. From the appearance of the large extent of bushes browsed, it was concluded that the horse lived till some time in March. None of the rest of the horses were ever heard of. Mr. Willey, not liking his situation in Bartlett, sold his land there soon after the loss of his horse and purchased an original right in Conway, where he lived an independent farmer until his death on the 14th of June, 1844, at the age of ninety-one years, being the last original male inhabitant of that town. An anecdote of him is considered worth relating here. Owing to the scarcity of provisions among the early settlers and the vigilance of the hunters, moose and deer soon became scarce; but bears remained numerous for a long time and are yet somewhat plenty. These animals often proved an intolerable nuisance to the farmers, destroying their sheep, hogs, and other creatures.

One night in the summer of 1800, Mr. Willey was waked from his sleep by the noise of his sheep running furiously by his house. Springing from his bed to a window, he discovered by the light of the moon, an enormous bear in close pursuit of them. Calling his eldest son, instantly, then a stout boy about fourteen years old, they sallied forth with their gun, and nothing on but their night clothes, to pursue this fell destroyer. By this time the sheep had made a turn and were coming pell-mell toward the house with the bear at their heels. Secreting themselves a moment until the sheep had passed, Mr. Willey sprang forth with his gun to salute his ursalean majesty. Old bruin, stopping to see what his ghostly visitor meant, was instantly fired at and severely wounded. Mr. Willey and his boy, with their axes, offered him a closer combat, and he readily accepted the challenge. After two or three charges they considered it the better part of valor to retreat to the house, which they did, closely pursued by the bear. While they were in the house reloading their gun, the enraged animal went round to a back window, through which he endeavored to enter the house, to be revenged of his antagonists. The room adjoining being dark, and Mrs. Willey supposing the bear to be on the other side of the house, in attempting to look out through the window, put her head within a few inches of his nose. On discovering her perilous situation, she gave one of those piercing female shrieks which make the welkin ring, and fell back on the floor. By this time they had reloaded their gun and now issued forth to renew the combat. But owing to the bad state of the powder, they were unable to fire the gun again. Perceiving the bear to be gaining strength, and now showing signs of an intention to retreat to the woods, after a few moments' consultation they determined to make another desperate effort to kill him with their axes. Mr. Willey, after receiving strong assurances from his boy that he would stand by him, approached the bear a second time, and by one well directed blow on his head, felled him to the ground.

After passing Conway you will come into Bartlett, and I will give you some account of the early settlements there as I received it from Richard Garland, Esq., in his eighty-second year. His intellect and memory are good now in his advanced age, and he says that in December, 1783, he was one inhabitant among five who came into that location, and that there were but few inhabitants for a distance of thirty-six miles, mostly woods, seventy-five miles from Dover, where they had to go for their provisions; and then they had them to draw on a hand-sleigh, in the winter, over a little bushed path, without a bridge. The people in Conway, when the streams were open, went down the Saco river in boats, or rather canoes, which they made out of a large tree by digging it out and making it large enough to carry several hundred weight, and when they came to a place where the falls prevented their passing, they would unlade their boats and carry their provisions and boats until they came to a smooth place again. At one time the inhabitants got out of provisions and sent for new supplies, and there came on a heavy rain, and the Saco river was risen to that height they could not get back for some time, and those they left of their families had to stint themselves to live on seven potatoes per diem until their return with provisions.

After some years this Mr. Garland had got a small piece of land cultivated, and it then needed plowing, and two of his neighbors offered him a team if he could get a plow; he then went seven miles and borrowed the nearest one in the morning, brought it home on his back, and his neighbor used it for him, while he, the same day, did a great day's work at piling timber. At noon, he went one and a half miles and bought fifty pounds of hay to feed his team on, and this hay he carried home on his back; at night he carried this same plow home on his own back, which made him thirty-one miles, and half the distance with a load, beside doing a good day's work, and then, as he says, was welcomed to partake of the bounties which a kind wife had provided, and then could sit down in their humble cot with her and their family of young children, without fear or trouble. As they at that period began to raise enough to support their families, they had only seventeen miles to go to mill, and in the winter God provided them with a good bridge of ice, and in the summer they crossed the Saco river in canoes. His family in those days, as the old gentleman says, was a happy one; but he did not realize it then as he now does, while he can look back to that time when he would work hard all day, and at night come in and take his supper; then he would in the evening return to his work, and his wife, after putting her children to rest, would go out with him and pick up the small brush and keep him a good light to work by, until nine o'clock. She then would go in and make them a cup of tea, which they could partake of together, and then they could retire to rest, happy in their humble engagements, trying to get an honest living.

In 1790, in the month of June, Pequaket being incorporated into towns, Bartlett was incorporated under Governor Bartlett and called after his name. In August,

they had a town meeting and chose town officers. Jonathan
Tasker, first selectman; John Pendexter, second; Thomas
Spring, third; Richard Garland, first constable and col-
lector of taxes in Bartlett. The next winter they had a
school. Moses Bigelow was the first teacher of this school
of about fifteen scholars; now they have their large schools,
which will average in the year 1844 over one hundred and
fifty scholars, and they have one hundred and fifty voters
in this small valley amidst these mountains. There was a
time when one of these inhabitants had got entirely out
of meat and came to this Mr. Garland for some to carry
into the woods, while he went and found some moose to
make meat for his family. Mr. Garland gave him half he
had himself, and then the man steered along for the
woods, and in a few days he returned as rich as any man
could be, seemingly, with news of having killed eight
moose, fine and fat. He then gave Mr. Garland three hundred pounds of this meat, provided he would take a hand-
sleigh and go bring it in, which he did, and he now says
that a bigger man never need be than he was then with
this supply, great as it was, of meat.

As they had begun to make a road, some people in
Portland offered to give any man a barrel of rum if he
would get it up through the Notch. Captain Rosebrook
volunteered his services and went to Bartlett with his
horse and car, and on the other side of the Saco made a
raft, rolled on this proffered barrel, then stood in water
up to his knees, and with a long pole pushed it across.
He then, with the assistance of others, this Mr. Garland
was one, put it upon his car and carried it up through
the Notch, at least as much of it as was left through the
politeness of those who helped manage the affair. This was
the first article brought up through where the road goes

Getting a team up the rocks at the Notch

Hamstringing a moose at Sawyer's Rock

Carrying a lady down Jacob's Ladder

now, and the first article of loading ever brought down, was a barrel of tobacco, raised in Lancaster by one Titus Brown, and the road was so crooked they were forced to cross the stream, as Mr. Garland says, thirty-two times to get from Bartlett to the top of the Notch, where now is the Notch House and the post-office, where Thomas J. Crawford now lives. The first white child born in Conway was Jeremiah Lovejoy, eighty-two years ago. Leaving Conway you will pass along through Bartlett till you come to Hart's Location. This was located to Thomas Chadbourne by Governor Wentworth, under the crown of Great Britain, for services rendered by Chadbourne in the old Indian wars, and was called Chadbourne's Location. Chadbourne sold it to Richard Hart for fifteen hundred dollars, and then the name was changed to Hart's Location. Then you will come against Sawyer's Rock, which comes down near the river so that there is just room for the road. This derived its name from the circumstance of Nash and Sawyer,[14] when they first were bushing the path for a horse to travel in through the Notch; they got down as far as here, and camped for the night, and in the morning they emptied their junk bottle of its contents, and Sawyer broke it against the rock and gave it the name of Sawyer's Rock, and it has ever since borne that name. And this was the first temperance meeting on the Saco river, or, so far as my remembrance is concerned, in history in the White Mountains.

Some time after this there were two men riding on horseback by the names of Blake and Moulton, and they saw near the rock two moose at play. They sprang from their horses and frightened them. They attempted to jump the rock, but the men, having the advantage, caught one of them by the hind leg, and with a jack-knife, cut off his heel cords and hamstrung him. They then went up and cut his throat. As they were travelers and had not the means of saving the meat, they went down to Bartlett and gave it to the inhabitants, who were glad to receive it. This happened, Father thinks, forty years ago.

There are in this Location eight voters and twenty-six children under sixteen years of age, and they had a school-house built in 1844. It accommodates only four families, on account of the distance they live apart, and the rest have to board their children from home if they give them a chance for a school.

Then you will come up to my father's. Here the stage stops and changes horses. Here the traveler may stop for a time, if he chooses, as Mr. Davis, last season, made a horse path from his house to the top of Mount Washington. This was done with considerable expense to him, and for no other reason than to accommodate those who might prefer going from there on the mountains, as they had several fine views in going that way. He charges the same as others do for guiding travelers up the mountains. Gentlemen and ladies also can ascend. Then you will, after leaving Father's, come to what is called the old Notch House, which place was settled, Uncle William says, about fifty-three years ago by one Mr. Davis, who first began there; since which period, others have lived there for a short time until Samuel Willey bought the place and repaired it. He with his family lived there till that dreadful night in August when all were destroyed by the great storm, described in the foregoing pages; then John Pendexter built the barn, and that stands there still, and he improved it. Others have lived there, by turns, until last season Mr. Fabyan made thorough repairs, both on the house and stable, and this season he has built a new frame for a house, seventy feet by forty, for himself, so that by next season, he may be prepared for company that, visiting the mountains, wish to spend a portion of their time at the Willey House. This place, which is now nothing but sand and gravel, was over a beautiful valley, covered with maple, and there used to be a great quantity of sugar made there. Then you will come up through the Notch to Thomas Crawford's, called the Notch House. He has a road to the mountain, nearly in the same place I first traveled, which was the first path ever made to the top of Mount Washington. You will pass along to where a man and his wife were once traveling, with one horse, in what used to be called a pung, and met in their way a moose. The snow was deep, and he, thinking he had a right to his path, refused to turn out; but when they came near, the moose jumped over the whole concern and just cleared the woman's head.

Then from the Notch four miles will bring you to the old Rosebrook stand, where once stood, in or near the road, a shed seventy feet long. As some hunters were pursuing a moose, he came into the road and went directly through this shed, passed on by the house and made for the river, and went down the falls, dislocating one of his knee joints. The hunters followed about three miles, caught him, and made a grand feast of him. It was in those days no uncommon thing to find these animals at any time when they were hunted for.

This ancient Rosebrook place is thirty-six miles from Conway, eighteen from Lancaster, eighteen from Franconia, and a good road we now have over Cherry Mountain, where once was a good turnpike, and it may be traveled with safety both summer and winter toward Jefferson. This place, also, is eighteen miles from Littleton, and stages run six times a week alternately, coming from Conway Mondays, Thursdays, and Saturdays, resting on Sundays, and arrive at either place, at night, fifty-four miles apart. When you get to the old Rosebrook place, you are in the most romantic scenery, perhaps, this side of the mountains.

The reader may suppose me partial to this place, and well he may, as I have lived here so long and have seen good times with my friends, who extend all over the land in every direction; from this place, also, we have a good horse path to Trinity Height, the summit of Mount Washington. Nearly seven miles of this road is over a comparatively level surface, and two and one-quarter miles is on rising ground; and many have seated themselves on a horse at the house, and never dismounted until they have been to the top of the mountain and returned. This can be accomplished in six to nine hours. Parties often stop by the way and fish for trout. These in old times were plenty, and of large size; but in this day, having so many fishing for them, they do not have time to grow very large before they are called for. But they are excellent, although small. Trout is the only kind of fish caught in these cold streams about the hills, and not much game is left excepting deer, which live here yet, and are caught now and then by having good dogs to find and follow them until tired out; sometimes the dog kills them, sometimes the hunter. Sometimes they are driven to the meadow, sometimes to the pond, where they are hunted after in canoes, and taken or killed.

As in the providence of God, everything changes in this world, the weather now is not so cold as it formerly was. We have now scarcely a week of steady cold, when, in former times, I have heard grandmother say she has seen six weeks at a time that neither the heat from her log cabin nor the sun would soften the snow so much as to cause one drop of water to fall from the eaves of the house. We now seldom have over two feet of snow at a time, and in years past it was no uncommon thing to have from six to nine feet. I have seen nine feet measured upon a level surface, and have known the snow to fall in less than twenty-four hours, twenty-seven inches. Yet we have early and late frosts in the spring and early frosts in the fall, which prevent our raising such things as the frost injures; but we generally can raise good oats and potatoes, and sometimes wheat, rye, and peas. In 1820, I raised some sound corn, but have never since had any get ripe. There is not a better place in New England for cattle and sheep than this. Goats and mules would do well, but they are too troublesome.

We can now go to Portland and back with a team in from six to eight days; in old times, it has taken twenty-two days to go from Lancaster to Portland, and back. The snow was so deep at one time that they were obliged to leave their horses seven days in one place before they could be moved. The average time of snow in the fall is about the first of November, and it goes off, generally, the first of April, so that about the middle of May, we here begin to plow and prepare our ground for raising such things as the climate will permit. Fowls do well here, such as ducks, geese, chickens; and the turkey here is excellent. We have kept pigeons, but they never seemed to increase to do much, only serving to amuse the children. Bees do well here and are common in the woods. They make the best flavored honey, as they have such a variety of wild flowers to extract their sweets from. As for pork, we do not raise enough here to support our own families, but depend on buying, principally, for our own use. There is some maple sugar made in different places about these mountains, but little in comparison to what there was in former times. And the probable amount of trout caught from one year to another, according to my judgment, in the Amanoosuc and Saco rivers, is from six to seven hundred weight. The average weight is from four ounces to eight. There have been some caught here, forty years ago, that would weigh four and five pounds, and many and large ones now are found in the vicinity, in several directions. And salmon have been taken here, fifty years since, of ten pounds weight. Three or four hundred different Alpine White Mountain plants are found about here, and there are still found on some of the slides near the Willey, or old Notch, House, handsome minerals or crystallized quartz. There used to be great quantities of fur taken around these mountains, but wild animals have all been hunted so much they are getting to be scarce; but there are some sable, or martin, and some few other animals caught every year.

I will give the minutes of the weather:

1844.	Sunrise.	2 p.m.	Sunset.	1845.	Sunrise.	2 p.m.	Sunset.
July 22	38	87	60	January 30	*8	10	*4
" 23	67	78	66	" 31	15	*1	*5
" 24	49	79	60	February 1	*22	*2	*21
" 25	52	66	51	" 2	*33	*6	*12
" 26	38	70	56	" 3	*34	*8	*6
" 27	28	68	56	" 4	*2	10	4
" 28	30	78	54	" 5	20	18	14
" 29	54	78	63	" 6	6	2	2
" 30	50	71	64	" 7	2	4	1
" 31	64	66	58	" 8	*1	6	3

*Below zero.

This is the register of the thermometer for A.D. 1844–5, when, on the whole, we had a moderate winter for this part of the country, and the summers, in general, are not so warm as they were formerly. As the land is cleared, perhaps the winds in summer have greater range, render the atmosphere more pleasant; and in winter, snow that used to fall upon the stumps and bushes, and all level places, is blown off by the winds, and there is generally a cooler, more dry, and salubrious air.

[Mr. Crawford moved to Guildhall, Vermont, in 1837, where he lived till 1843 when he rented the house about one half mile north of his former mountain home. Here he remained until 1846 when a fever set in and, in connection with his former complaints, death bore him to that home "from whence no traveler returns." For nearly twenty-five years he had resided in that secluded and romantic spot, so well known at the present day as the old Crawford place.

Mr. Crawford was well adapted to a mountain life, being a stout athletic man with a great share of courage and fortitude. Although rough in his outward appearance he possessed a kind heart, and no man was more ready or willing to administer to the distressed or suffering or to aid in difficulty than Ethan Allen Crawford was, in former days almost as universally known to the pleasure traveling community as the White Hills themselves. His giant strength will long be remembered by those who have been carried down the ragged sides of Mount Washington upon his huge shoulders before a path was made suitable for a horse to ascend. As a guide, all felt secure while under his care. Every locality was known to him and everything which was of interest to the tourist was pointed out with pleasure by him. Without his presence the White Hills to many lost half their charms.]

CHAPTER XI

———

Dennis Stanley's success at moose hunting.
McIntire's ride down the Notch.
Israel's river. John's river. Amanoosuc river.
Pemegewasset river. Saco river. Peabody's river.

ONE of the early settlers in the regions of the mountains by the name of Stanley devoted a considerable portion of his time in the fall and winter following the trail of moose and deer. He at one time was out of meat as well as that luxury which is so freely used at the present day to the destruction of peace and happiness in too many families. In order to supply his family with food and to raise means to purchase something to keep his *spirits* up, he one morning, alone, started off with gun in hand for Cherry Pond, knowing that moose frequently resorted there. His gun had, by long usage, got so as to prime itself when the powder was emptied into the barrel. Soon after his arrival at the pond he struck his camp-fire and set down to indulge himself with his pipe and tobacco, when he heard the tread of moose in the water; he stepped carefully out of his camp and beheld five of them wading in the shallow water upon the edge of the pond; they were apparently about to cross to the opposite shore as they were making for the deep water, all in single file; no time was to be lost, and Stanley seized his powder horn and uncorked it, then taking several bullets from his pouch he put them into his mouth and waited till the foremost

moose was nearly immersed in water, when he waded into
the water and took a position so as to prevent the moose
from crossing the pond. Upon his appearance in sight of
the animals, as he had anticipated, they chose to return
back rather than attempt to cross the pond. In their retreat the same order was observed, except reversed, and
as Stanley's position was at right angles from them, and
the foremost in their retrograde movement being within
a few rods, a discharge from his gun laid him rolling in
the water. The powder horn was immediately applied to
the muzzle of the gun, a bullet followed from his mouth
with the alacrity which an old experienced hunter only
knows, and the second moose was lying dead near the
first one; the gun was again reloaded and discharged until
the blood of all five of the moose was mingling with the
water; this was considered a good day's work, it being
early in the season when it is difficult to catch them.
Moose are seldom hunted at the present day until late in
the winter or early in the spring when the snow has become deep and a crust formed upon its surface, so as to
impede their progress in running. In early time they were
very plenty about the valleys at the base of the White
Mountains, and were extensively hunted by many solely
for their hides and tallow, and the nose, which is considered by the epicure as excelled only by the beaver's
tail as a luxury. Such numbers of them were to be found
in those days that an old professional hunter by the name
of Caswell succeeded in killing ninety-nine in one season
and oftentimes leaving them without taking off their hides.
A period of fifty years has exterminated and driven them
almost entirely from this section of the county. Occasionally signs of them are to be seen about Pond Safety, lying
a few miles to the north of the White Mountains, but sel-

dom are they taken except in the northerly part of the county. Deer are still to be found quite plenty in all the towns lying upon the northerly side of the hills and afford much amusement to young hunters during the winter season.

As in all new settlements, with a small clearing occasionally dotted from the huge forest, neighbors miles apart, most of their food composed of the coarsest fare, in times of want of assistance compelled to resort to the brain for ways and means as a substitute, forms a condition in life for resolution and courage as well as vigorous minds and muscular strength.[1] At one time a company of teamsters on their way to Portland with their pork, produce, and other articles to be exchanged for West India goods, as was customary in those days, traveled over the Notch road. As they were gliding along, singing cheerfully, down one of the long and steep hills in the Notch, the road being filled from the great amount of travel with what is termed cradle-holes, the sleigh of a Mr. McIntire in passing through one of these holes received so sudden a jerk as to break the pole or tongue of his sleigh; seated upon the front part of his load, his presence of mind was not for a moment lost; although quite a number of teams were close upon him, he immediately put one of his feet against one of his horses, the other foot against the other horse, holding the sleigh from off the heels of his horses, kept on his way in this manner until he arrived at the bottom of the hill in safety. After reaching level ground, the axe, which in those times was seldom missed from the side of a teamster's load, was applied to a small green tree, a new pole soon substituted in the place of the broken one, and away glided the happy train, causing the forest to echo from the merry laughter upon McIntire's improvement on hold-backs.

Maine, New Hampshire, Vermont, Massachusetts, and Connecticut each are beholden to the White Hills for a portion of the water which flows over their soil. Upon the northerly and westerly sides of the hills Israel's river, John's river, and the Amanoosuc all take their rise. Israel's river passes through the towns of Jefferson and Lancaster, emptying into the Connecticut at Lancaster. Its supply of water is sufficient for the use of various mills and machinery both at Jefferson and Lancaster. It is rapid and receiving its supply as it does from the mountains, it requires but little rain to cause it to overflow its banks. The Indian name of this stream was Sinoogawnock.[2] It received its present name from an old man by the name of Israel Glines, who hunted and fished about and in its waters previous to any settlement along its borders.

John's river takes its rise in the valley at the base of Mounts Washington and Adams about three miles south of Israel's river;[3] a ridge of high land running from Mount Adams separates the waters of the two streams; it passes nearly the whole length of the town of Whitefield and discharges itself into the Connecticut at Dalton, about seven miles below the mouth of Israel's river. It derived its name from a brother of Israel's by the name of John Glines and who chose this stream for his hunting and fishing grounds.

The Amanoosuc is formed from the various little brooks running south of the former rivers but a few miles. Standing upon the summit of Mounts Washington, Clay, or Adams, all of the tributaries to the above mentioned rivers can be distinctly seen winding their course through the dense forest for miles, resembling foot paths at a distance. The Amanoosuc passes through the towns of Carroll, Bethlehem, Littleton, Lisbon, Bath, emptying into the Connecticut at Wells River, nearly twenty-five miles south of the outlet of John's river.

On the southwest of this range of mountains the tributaries of the Pemegewasset spring out at different points, mingling together until they unite with the Merrimack.

As you travel to the eastward the Saco river claims a passing notice; one of its principal branches takes its rise at the head of the Notch, and enclosed upon both banks by high mountains for several miles it is, in a wet season, one of the most rapid and mad streams to be found throughout the whole northern country.

Still farther to the eastward is to be found a crazy little stream known as Peabody's river. The origin of this stream we copy from J. H. Spaulding's *Historical Relics of the White Mountains.*

"The father of Oliver Peabody, who resided at Andover, Mass., in one of his excursions into New Hampshire met with an adventure which has connected his name with the geography of the country, and which, for that reason, as well as its singularity, may, perhaps, with propriety, be mentioned here. He was passing a night in the cabin of an Indian, situated on the height between the Saco and the Androscoggin rivers. The inmates of this rude dwelling were awakened in the course of the night by a loud noise, and had scarcely time to escape, before the hut was swept away by a torrent of water rushing impetuously down the hill. On reconnoitring the spot, they found that this torrent had burst out suddenly from a place where there was no spring before." This is supposed to date back to the origin of the branch of Peabody river, that runs in front of the Glen House, and hence came its name.[4]

This stream finds an outlet in the Androscoggin in the town of Gorham.

CHAPTER XII

First death upon the mountains.
Death of Lizzie Bourne.
Death of Benjamin Chandler.
White Mountains Hotels. Natural curiosities.

LATE in the fall of 1851 a young Englishman[1] arrived at
the Notch House and was desirous to ascend to the
summit of Mount Washington. Beyond vegetation snow
had capped the hills, and it was considered a dangerous
undertaking, and the young man was so informed by the
landlord. But all argument failed to discourage him in his
rashness, and at last a guide consented to accompany
him, supposing that after a few miles travel his friend
would become tired and give up the idea. They proceeded
as far as the top of Mount Clinton, a keen sharp wind was
meeting them directly in the face, and as they ascended
the snow became deeper, and the guide again halted and
informed the Englishman of the danger they were in. But
the young man, like many others, relying upon his own
inexperience, was determined not to turn back until his
anticipations had been realized. The guide, knowing it to
be an impossibility to reach the top and again return before night, turned his face toward home, supposing the
young tourist would, when left alone, retrace his steps.
After the guide returned home night soon followed, but
not the Englishman. The following morning a party of
hardy men started in pursuit. Arriving at the top of Mount

Clinton, his track was traced to the summit. It was supposed that he intended to take a more direct course than
the route he went up, as he soon diverged from the path.
By this step his descent became much more hazardous,
and they had not followed his track but a short distance
before discovering that he had fallen several times over
precipices, and also showing [sic] signs of fatigue. Blood,
soon after, was discovered, and the party hurried along,
feeling the utmost anxiety for his fate, until they struck
upon the valley of the Amanoosuc, where they found him
with his face lying in a little stream, his body badly mangled and nearly naked. Fatigue, bruises, and cold had
prevented him from going farther, and he lay down and
perished.

The afternoon of September 13, 1855, at two o'clock,
Mr. George W. Bourne and daughter, with Miss Lizzie
Bourne, niece of the above gentleman and only daughter
of E. E. Bourne of Kennebunk, Maine, left the Glen House
to walk to the summit without a guide.* At the time of
their starting the sun was pouring her clear and soft au-
tumnal rays over the valley through which this little party
had to pass, although a dark and heavy cloud had been
noticed to hang over the summit during the early part of
the day. As they proceeded up the ravine, occasionally
casting a glance at "Tip-Top," how joyous were their anticipations; the forests echoing back the merry songs and
peals of laughter as they crossed the little bridge with
their white handkerchief suspended upon a short staff,
waving in triumph of their success. Alas! how little did
they think what a day or an hour might bring forth, or

*[For] the particulars of the death of Miss Bourne and Mr. Chand-
ler we are indebted to J. H. Spaulding of the "Tip-Top House."
[Lucy Crawford's footnote.]

how soon their happiness was to be exchanged for extreme sufferings both to mind and body. When within about two miles of the top, the black cloud which had been hovering over the summit began to settle down the mountain side, and soon their apparel became drenched, rendering it extremely hard and difficult for them to ascend over the rough and rugged path; darkness soon enveloped them, and with no knowledge of the route, they were left to grope their way in fear and silent meditation. That evening was a fearful one to those stopping at the summit houses,[2] for the dense clouds had made it necessary to light the lamps at an early hour, and the winds with a voice like thunder made the mountain top tremble. Rev. L. L. Eastman and lady, of Littleton, were the only visitors at the Tip-Top House on that lonely eve, they not being able to descend on that day from the heavy mist which enshrouded the top the whole day. These two strangers with the inmates of the house were comfortably seated around the fire, listening to the mournful dirges of the roaring winds without, little dreaming that suffering and death lay almost at their very door. "Early," (says Mr. Spaulding) "did they retire to rest, with the lifting storm to rock us, and the loud wind to sing our lullaby." Nothing disturbed their slumbers until a little before daybreak, when a rap upon the outer door aroused the inmates. Upon going out, faint glimmerings of light began to appear in the distant east and, by the rays, two shivering mortals, a father and daughter, were seen standing before the door, their dress sparkling with frost—the thermometer being down to twenty-nine degrees. Night had changed the scene upon the mountain top—a calm had succeeded the howling winds of the preceding evening, not a cloud was to be seen save the mist sleeping over distant waters. Soon the sad tale was told of the sufferers standing before the door, and of the almost certainty of death a little farther down the mountain.

A faint hope that life might not be extinct caused no delay in hurrying to the spot where Lizzie Bourne lay with her head supported upon a stone. Imagination cannot paint the scene! Pen cannot describe the feelings of those who went to render aid! Her hair wildly flying over her face was carefully brushed aside, when her piercing eyes, fixed in death, caused a shudder to pass over the stout and hardy forms of those whom duty had called to the spot. Her cheeks had assumed a pale and death-like hue and were as cold as the unfeeling stones around her. Her body was carried to the Summit House and every means resorted to by the good Samaritans for the space of three hours to excite the blood and restore circulation, but all efforts availed nothing. Death had chilled her veins, stopped all pulsation of that once warm heart and sealed her lips forever.

It appeared, by the finding of Mr. Bourne's staff and a small pile of stone which he had thrown together as a protection, against the cold winds, to the young ladies, that they had been within *nineteen* rods of the house, then retraced their steps twenty-one rods, when exhausted nature compelled them to halt, and poor Lizzie lay down to sleep her last sleep. Help was sent for, her body placed upon a rude soldier's bier, prayer offered by Rev. L. L. Eastman, and silently and solemnly she was borne down the rocks towards her sad and last resting place. Almost every visitor to the summit, as they pass by the lone spot, stop and add to the mound another stone in memento of her sad fate.

The following is copied from the register at the Summit

House. Reports have gone forth attaching blame to the landlords, but the language set forth by the pen of Mr. Bourne must correct all such statements.

Tip-Top Mt. Washington

Sept. 14. George W. Bourne & daughter—Miss Lizzie Bourne, daughter of E. E. Bourne Esq. of Kennebunk, Me.

Miss Lizzie Bourne perished by cold on the mountain, they having missed their way in consequence of darkness; the night was very windy and cold and all three came near perishing. They left the Glen House at 2 o'clock on Thursday and arrived at this house (Tip Top) Friday morning at early daylight.

We shall ever feel ourselves under a debt of gratitude that we can never repay, for the sympathy manifested by the good people of the Summit House to us, and for their unceasing exertion to restore the young lady to life. There is One higher who will abundantly reward them for every good act.

No act falls fruitless,
None can tell how great its power may be—
God is with all who love the right
And serve him in simplicity.
G. W. Bourne & daughter

Sept. 14

By the Providence of God we have the sad pleasure of being present to witness the consequence of the tragedy recorded above, and also to be participaters in extending aid and sympathy to those involved. With pleasure we record the acknowledgment that the Keepers of the Summit House did all, that, under the circumstances, could be done for the living and the dead.

Rev. L. L. Eastman & wife

The 4th of August, 1856, Benjamin Chandler, a resident of Wilmington, Delaware, left that city with the intention of visiting the New England states and spending a short time among their hills and mountains. On the 7th of August he arrived at the Glen House and late in the afternoon of that day with a small bundle under his arm left for the summit. As the sun was about to take its departure, two gentlemen (both ministers) passed him with their guide on the way to the Tip-Top. Upon their arrival they informed the landlords, Spaulding and Hall, of the fact, and as he had ascended only about halfway, they had some fears that he could not reach the top without assistance, it then being nearly nine o'clock in the evening. After waiting about an hour, and Mr. Chandler not making his appearance, a guide was dispatched down the bridle path to render assistance if needed. The guide returned after a while, stating that he could get no trace of him, although he called at the top of his voice at intervals but received no answer. The wind was blowing cold from the northwest, and a dense cloud lay upon Tip-Top, pouring out its watery contents. The guide lost his light by the strong wind, and when he returned his clothes were completely saturated with rain. The conclusion of the people at the summit was that as he could not be made to hear the voice of the guide he must have turned back and sought shelter at the Ledge at the terminus of the carriage road, and where some workmen upon the road were camping. Next morning a search was made, but no tidings of him could be learned nor any trace where he could have stopped through the long dismal night. Time passed along, and the mystery remained unveiled until late in September, when a gentleman arrived making enquiries in regard to the old gentleman who had so suddenly disappeared. It was a Mr. David Chandler, son of Benjamin, in search of his missing father. He, before leaving, offered a reward of five hundred dollars for any information that would lead to his discovery.

Since, it has been ascertained that the old gentleman

was seventy-five years of age, active in his habits, having for nearly fifty years been connected with the Masonic Fraternity, and possessed a fortune of one hundred thousand dollars.

A report that an old gentleman had been seen down on the old Fabyan road at Brabrook's[3] stable on the 8th or 9th of August who inquired the way to Gibb's,[4] and also that a voice late at night at Gibb's, coming from the mountain with a cry of help, had led search to be made almost entirely upon the westerly side of the mountains, and more particularly on Mount Clinton.

On Sunday, July 19, 1857, a visitor to the summit, while rambling over the rocks and precipices, discovered the skeleton of a man on the northerly side of a ledge that forms the top of the first high point, eastward, about half a mile from the summit. He had evidently lost the path, being nearly thirty rods from the traveled path, and to shelter himself from the cold winds and storm, had crawled under the shelving side of this high rock to sleep his last sleep. At the time of the discovery very little flesh remained upon one arm and shoulder and upon the side of his neck and face; a few gray hairs also hung to the skull. The feet, hands, one leg, and one bone of the arm were gone and could not be found. Since that time a leg was found not far distant from where the rest of the bones lay when first discovered. His ribs had nearly all been gnawed off, his boots and stockings gone. The wildcat, which roams the summit, had evidently caused the destruction of bones. Among the mass of worm-moving rags lay a gold watch, which had ceased its ticking at a quarter before eleven o'clock. The remains were gathered together and upon the back of a pack-horse forwarded to the Glen to await the arrival of his son. The lone spot where this sad occurrence took place was about one hundred rods to the east of where Lizzie Bourne, under almost the same circumstances, shared a similar fate.[5]

One of the many objects of interest at all summer resorts is good Hotels. After a long day's ride, a pleasant and comfortable room with an accommodating landlord, a large share of the fatigue of the journey is soon forgotten. The large and elegant Houses about the mountains add much towards gratifying the pleasure-seeking tourist. As you approach the mountains upon the westerly side, the White Mountain House, kept by Mr. Brabrook, first meets the eye; about five miles below, at the head of the Notch, stands the new and elegant Hotel, known as the Notch House, and kept by Gibbs & Co. Upon the opposite side of the mountains stands the large and spacious House known as the Glen House and kept by Thomson.[6] The Summit Houses, kept by Hall & Co., are all that can be desired, when considering the difficulty of erecting upon such a site. Every piece of timber, every board, as well as all the other materials were carried up a distance of seven or eight miles, either upon the forward wheels of a wagon or upon the back of a horse, and at a time when the path would hardly be considered suitable for a person on foot to travel.

At the Franconia mountains two spacious Hotels have been erected; one near the Old Man of the Mountain, the other upon the road near to where the path turns off to go to the Flume, and known as the Flume House. These constitute the principal Houses in the immediate vicinity of the mountains.

The various curiosities about this range of hills are so numerous as to render it impossible to enumerate them; the eye finds at almost every step something new to gaze

upon. As you pass along upon the banks of the Amanoosuc on the westerly side of the mountains, many beautiful
little cascades and rivulets come tumbling down from the
sides of the small but ragged mountains and continue to
increase in magnitude as well as in number as you approach the Notch. The Notch itself runs from the northwest to the southeast and is nearly three miles in length,
through the narrowest part. In passing down this huge
gulf you behold a boundless feast of natural curiosities
and the most romantic scenery extant. High upon the side
of Mount Willard a small dark hole is seen, which appears
but a minute speck in the solid rock. Several attempts
were made to reach its entrance, but so steep were the
overhanging and ragged cliffs that all efforts proved fruitless. In 1850 a Mr. Franklin Leavitt, a resident of Lancaster, succeeded in the undertaking; a rope was attached
around his body and he was let down from the top of the
cliff, dangling in the air till he came to the entrance of this
large and dark cavern. With all his dare-devil spirit, upon
reaching the mouth, the bones lying promiscuously around
daunted his courage, and he refused to enter, and as a
signal to be drawn up he kicked the rope and was resting
again upon a more solid footing. This den since its discovery by the old veteran Crawford has been known by the
appellation of the Devil's Den. As it would be a difficult
task even for his satanic majesty to reach its entrance,
reason teaches us to think that birds of prey have chosen
this secluded spot to make their repast and rear their
young unmolested.[7]

Nearly opposite to the Devil's Den, standing upon a
small bridge and casting your eye upon the side of the
mountain, you behold that mountain stream termed the
Silver Cascade. Almost as far as the eye can reach the

water is seen gliding over precipice after precipice, occasionally hid by some over-hanging trees or projecting cliff, but soon appearing again in all its splendor; as the eye follows it along down the hill the fall appears more rapid, apparently sliding over the smooth surface of huge ledges, at times bounding away over boulders, foaming as if anxious to reach some serener basin wherein to rest; nearer and nearer it dashes along until it discharges its fury into the Saco river.

About one-half mile to the east still another cascade is seen, although not so attractive as the Silver Cascade. The distance which it is to be seen is about three hundred feet, and the appearance is quite different from the above described one, there being but three precipices over which it leaps; as it glides along over two of them it is quiet, then dividing, passing over the third in three distinct currents, uniting again at the bottom where it is received into a beautiful basin.

Upon the easterly side of the mountains they are not without their share of similar curiosities. A pleasant walk from the Glen brings you to Glen Ellis Falls. These falls are but a few rods from the road on Ellis river, and the height of the fall is about eighty feet.

There is, about one mile from this romantic spot, still another cascade known as the Crystal Falls. The falls are about the same in distance as Glen Ellis but not so perpendicular. At one point its spray is thrown high into the air, and the next moment the water is quietly passing over smooth beds of moss, creating so much of a contrast that it seems as if nature had designed it expressly to gratify the eye.

The Gulf of Mexico[8] is also to be found upon the easterly side of the mountains. It is situated between Mount

Washington and Mount Adams, with Mount Clay as a backer on the west. The immense depth of this gulf can only be realized by standing upon the bank at the top and with the eye scan the deep abyss beneath.

Tuckerman's Ravine, on the opposite side of Mount Washington, is full of objects of interest calculated to enchant the traveler; Spaulding's Lake, the various slides and ragged cliffs projecting from every point, chain the eye of the tourist in wonder and amazement.[9]

The Franconia mountains, so called, belong to the range of White Hills; and to all lovers of the works of the Creator present many interesting scenes. The highest peak stands near the centre of the Franconia notch and is a little over 5,000 feet high. Many persons who have ascended Mount Lafayette consider the view from its summit equally as extensive as from the summit of Mount Washington. In passing through this Notch you are enclosed upon both sides of the road by a dense forest a distance of eight miles. A small clearing where the Notch House[10] is erected being the only one of any notice. One of the principal tributaries to the Pemegewasset river takes its rise near the height of land in this valley and courses along by the side of the road until you have reached the clearing, when it unites with other little streams rushing down from the different valleys below.

The Old Man of the Mountains is found among this group of hills. This curiosity is formed by huge rocks, and when standing at a certain point these rocks are so situated as to present the perfect outlines of the human face to the beholder; a few steps either way destroys the features, one by one, until nothing but a mass of ragged cliffs meets the eye. This curiosity is situated near the top of Mount Cannon, and by a circuitous route is accessible to the crown of his head. The storms of ages seem not to disturb the resting place of this stern old man, or cause a wrinkle to be furrowed upon his brow.

The next greatest object of attraction is the Flume. This romantic spot is located about one mile from the Flume House to the eastward. As you approach, and just before entering the Flume, you find the water gliding along over a smooth ledge a distance of more than one hundred feet and between thirty and forty feet in width, and although the water passes down rapidly, so smooth is the surface of the ledge that is almost resembles a still body of water; at the head of this ledge you pass into the Flume. This natural curiosity fills the beholder with amazement and admiration. As you stand at the mouth the chasm is seen for several hundred feet and grows narrower as you approach the upper end; at the outlet it is nearly twenty feet in width, while at the other end it is but about one-half that number of feet. The sides or walls are solid rock and from forty to fifty feet in height; near the centre of the flume an immense stone of several tons weight has at some former date rolled down from the cliffs far above and lodged a few feet from the top of the flume; and although made securely fast, it causes a person to shudder as he passes under it.[11] At all times there is quite a dampness as you pass through this fissure almost causing a chilly sensation to creep over the whole system; most of the ledge upon both sides is covered with moss and presents a cold dreary appearance even at noonday in summer.

The Pool and the Basin are also curiosities worthy of notice. The Pool is situated between the Basin and the Flume. The Basin is a deep chiseling in granite by the wearing waters for ages past and by the little rolling stones which have been swept down by the current. It is nearly forty feet in diameter and about one-half of that number of feet in depth. The small stones which are cast into this basin are so kept in motion as to constantly wear upon the bottom, and undoubtedly have aided much in wearing out this cavity. Similar pools and basins are to be found as you pass along by the side of the stream. So numberless are the lesser objects of curiosity that is is useless to attempt to describe them.

The wide-world renowned traveler, Bayard Taylor, in a late tour of the White Hills, thus describes his views of approaching the Mountains in a correspondence to the New York *Tribune*:

> I do not think any approach to the White Mountains can be more beautiful than that of the Saco Valley. You are carried so gently and with such sweetly prolonged surprises, into their heart—touched first, as it were, with their outstretched fingers, held awhile in their arms, and finally taken to their bosom. Their beauty wins before their sublimity awes you. On such an evening, with the depth of color increasing as the light fades, bars of alternate gold and violet flung from summits and through lateral gorges across the valley, and blue glimpses of stream or lake interrupting the rich, uniform green, every turn of the road gives you a new delight, every minute of the fleeting time is more precious than the last.
>
> Now, wherein is this scenery inferior to that of the Scotch Highlands, or the Lower Alps, or the Jura? In no respect to my eyes, but rather finer in its forms and combinations. To be sure, it lacks the magic of old associations; but this—if it be a defect —is one which is soon forgotten. The principal difference is one which applies to all American scenery. Virgin nature has a complete charm of its own; so has nature under subjection, cultivated, enriched, *finished* as a dwelling-place for man: but that transition state, which is neither one thing nor the other, gives an unsatisfactory impression in the midst of our highest enjoyment.

But few persons from abroad can know but little of the

beauties of the mountains during the season of autumn; it is only those who witness the scene day by day; a boundless scene of hill and dale, mountain and valley, with their sides dressed in gay and bright liveries, not in one somber-suited color, but all the variegated hues which the frosts are capable of putting upon the leaves of the different variety of trees; the tall pine, hemlock, and spruce peering up, each with a different shade of green, as if defying winter, while the maple, birch, and other hard wood growth have yielded up their summer dress for the yellow and sallow leaf before taking their departure to mingle with Mother Earth. Often, during this season of the year, while the sides of these hills present all the hues of the rainbow, their summits are capped with snow, presenting a scene of beauty and sublimity. The pen cannot describe, nor the brush of the skilful artists paint so beautiful a picture as nature has spread before us thoughout this mountainous country. Man, to realize and appreciate the beauties of this chain of Mountains, must first visit them. Neither can he learn them by riding over a railroad at lightning speed, or seated in a pent-up stage coach, catching a glance of their summits now and then, but he must pass over them and around them, seeking their most prominent cliffs and projections, for views in the beautiful valleys beneath. Time is also requisite—an hour, nor a day, is not sufficient to study this vast book of nature. While seated upon the summit of Mount Washington, all may be still and silent, a clear atmosphere, and the eye suffered to feast upon the country for miles around, while tomorrow how great the change—the valleys a dense sheet of fog—no object to be seen save the dense ocean, which to appearance, is spread before you, with here and there a mountain top peering above it in imitation of small islands.

So great has become the celebrity of the many objects of attraction about these hills that the walls of the parlors of private families are decorated with a painting of one or more of the most prominent curiosities—the windows in the cities of the principal venders of lithographic views are filled—and on the centre table stand the stereoscope, and lying by its side Tip-Top, the Cascades, and the many beautiful views which the artist has gathered.

CHAPTER XIII

———

Thermometrical tables for the years 1853-4.
Routes to the Mountains.
Towns about the Mountains.
Their accommodations for travelers.
Best views from surrounding towns.

THE following tables exhibit the difference of weather between 1844-5 and 1853-4. [Since the table for 1844-5 has been given on page 180 it is omitted here.]

The tables of the two latter years are copied from a small work published by J. H. Spaulding, who formerly kept the houses upon the summit.

During the long residence of the Crawfords at the Mountains but few persons ascended the summit except from the Crawford Houses. This consequently brought nearly all the travel to the Notch. Time has greatly facilitated the means of conveyance to the mountains, as well as creating new routes. By steam one can find himself upon either side of the White Hills he prefers and within a few miles of their base.

From Boston there are two different routes, one the eastern, the other the northern. From these two roads several other branches intersect. The route *via* Portland brings the tourist to Gorham, New Hampshire, and within eight miles of the base of the Mountains.

JUNE, 1853.   JULY, 1853.

Day.	Sunrise.	12 M.	Sunset.	Day.	Sunrise.	12 M.	Sunset
8	32	40	34	1	43	55	45
9	31	45	40	2	32	46	38
10	38	52	48	3	44	53	48
11	44	47	43	4	52	60	52
12	32	48	44	5	42	51	44
13	43	56	47	6	39	48	39
14	48	60	55	7	29	47	37
15	53	59	55	8	38	50	49
16	54	62	55	9	41	49	45
17	54	56	52	10	45	50	45
18	43	48	40	11	45	54	48
19	39	49	42	12	40	52	45
20	50	66	58	13	38	49	45
21	48	57	50	14	42	59	49
22	54	58	55	15	52	62	51
23	58	60	55	16	51	56	52
24	56	42	35	17	44	49	37
25	30	36	32	18	39	55	48
26	24	37	30	19	52	53	50
27	32	44	38	20	42	50	41
28	34	34	35	21	38	45	46
29	45	64	58	22	42	60	56
30	54	61	53	23	50	66	56
				24	54	64	59
				25	52	63	55
				26	50	51	45
				27	43	59	49
				28	39	47	45
				29	44	59	54
				30	49	59	56
				31	50	59	49

JUNE, 1854.   JULY, 1854.

Day.	Sunrise.	12 M.	Sunset.	Self-Register during night.	Day.	Sunrise.	12 M.	Sunset	Self-Register during night.
10	44	46	40	36	1	40	42	42	39
11	38	46	45	38	2	40	48	48	48
12	42	52	47	42	3	54	58	58	53
13	48	58	48	44	4	54	60	60	54
14	46	54	45	45	5	54	54	50	40
15	46	52	46	41	6	40	48	46	46
16	42	46	36	29	7	49	56	58	50
17	31	41	42	42	8	50	57	56	56
18	48	54	51	48	9	60	60	54	45
19	49	54	52	46	10	45	50	48	40
20	46	51	42	40	11	40	56	56	45
21	43	57	50	45	12	46	54	46	31
22	50	57	50	45	13	32	51	47	44
23	46	49	48	44	14	44	58	51	50
24	44	48	46	39	15	50	62	54	50
25	39	44	36	33	16	50	64	58	53
26	34	48	44	36	17	54	62	57	46
27	42	52	47	46	18	48	50	55	55
28	54	58	56	36	19	55	63	61	55
29	36	54	48	42	20	56	70	63	57
30	46	46	46	40	21	58	60	58	51
					22	52	62	58	52
					23	54	55	57	51
					24	53	56	54	54
					25	54	60	55	54
					26	56	60	54	39
					27	39	45	40	38
					28	41	50	49	45
					29	48	49	52	45
					30	47	48	44	40
					31	40	50	51	48

AUGUST, 1854.   SEPTEMBER, 1854.

Day.	Sunrise.	12 M.	Sunset.	Self-Register during night.	Day.	Sunrise.	12 M	Sunrise.	Self-Register during night.
1	50	61	56	52	1	48	52	50	
2	54	51	46	36	2	38	50	50	
3	38	40	45	44	3	51	52	51	
4	46	47	46	43	4	40	50	49	
5	45	56	54	47	5	54	60	59	
6	47	54	45	31	6	58	64	57	
7	33	38	36	32	7	52	49	42	
8	33	42	38	32	8	33	41	45	
9	34	66	48	36	9	46	45	43	
10	38	56	50	44	10	32	42	34	
11	45	60	54	49	11	32	46	46	
12	49	52	52	51	12	40	48	46	
13	52	54	51	33	13	30	40	45	
14	33	34	36	32	14	36	42	38	
15	41	47	45	44	15	40	40	32	
16	48	55	49	48	16	36			
17	48	55	48	46					
18	47	50	40	39					
19	39	58	48	44					
20	45	59	50	46					
21	46	50	48	40					
22	42	49	40	30					
23	30	54	52	50					
24	50	56	50	36					
25	36	40	38	38					
26	39	44	46	45					
27	46	44	38	39					
28	39	48	43	39					
29	39	56	60	48					
30	48	50	57	51					
31	51	56	60	48					

The length of days at the summit exceed those of the ocean's level by about forty minutes in the same latitude.

From Boston to Portland, - - - - - - - 105 miles.
   "   Portland to Alpine House, Gorham, N. H.,
        via Atlantic & St. Lawrence Railroad, -   91   "
   "   Alpine House to Glen House, at base of
        Mt. Washington, - - - - - - - -   8   "
        196 miles by Railroad, 8 miles by Stage, -   204   "

COCHECO ROUTE.

From Boston to Dover, via Boston & Maine Railroad,   68 miles.
   "   Dover to Alton Bay, - - - - - - -   28   "
   "   Alton Bay to Centre Harbor, by steamer, -   30   "
   "   Centre Harbor to Crawford House, - - -   56   "

    96 miles by Railroad, 30 by Steamer, 56 by Stage, 182   "

ROUTE via WEIRS AND CENTER HARBOR.

From Boston to Weirs, - - - - - - - - - 103 miles.
   "   Weirs to Centre Harbor, - - - - - -   10   "
   "   Centre Harbor to Conway, - - - - - -   30   "
   "   Conway to Crawford House, - - - - -   24   "

    103 miles by Railroad, 10 by Steamer, 54 by Stage, 167   "

In traveling over the Centre Harbor routes a pleasant excursion is made by steamer over the beautiful waters of the Winnipissiogee. "*The smile of the great Spirit*" will soon cheer up the drooping mind after a long, tedious, and monotonous ride in the dusty cars; a short trip from the landing at Centre Harbor on horseback brings you at the top of Red-Hill where the view of the placid sheet over which you have just sailed fully compensates for all the time and trouble.

FRANCONIA NOTCH ROUTE.

From Boston to Plymouth, N. H., by railroad, - - - 124 miles.
   "   Plymouth to Flume House, Franconia Notch, by stage, 24   "
   "   Flume House to Profile House, - - - - -   5   "
   "   Profile House to White Mountain House, - - -   26   "
   "   White Mountain House to Crawford House, - -   5   "
   "   Crawford House to Willey House, - - - - -   2   "

The above route is one that cannot fail to please all who desire a ride by the side of beautiful streams, bays, and lakes; immediately after getting clear of the dusty streets of the city you find the Merrimack gently gliding along by the side of the track, and soon the Winnipissiogee guides you to all its pretty bays until you arrive at the lake from which it takes its rise; a few miles again brings the cars upon the banks of the Pemegewasset following up its tributaries to the Flume House at the entrance of the Franconia notch.

ROUTE via WELLS RIVER AND LITTLETON, N.H.

From Boston to Wells River, - - - - - - -	162	miles.
" Wells River to Littleton, - - - - - - -	20	"
" Littleton to Crawford House, - - - - -	23	"
182 miles by Railroad, 23 by Stage, - - -	205	"

ROUTE via SEBAGO LAKE.

From Boston to Portland, - - - - - - - -	105	miles
" Portland to Standish, - - - - - - - -	16	"
" Standish to Bridgeton, by steamer, - - - -	28	"
" Bridgeton to Conway, - - - - - - - -	21	"
" Conway to Crawford House, - - - - - -	24	"
115 miles by Railroad, 51 by Stage, 28 by Steamer,	194	"

Gorham, through which the Atlantic & St. Lawrence Railroad[1] passes, is situated northeasterly of the mountains, and the Station House being but eight miles from the Glen House at the base of the mountains, travelers find less travel by stage upon this route than by any other. Although Gorham cannot be ranked among the productive towns of Coos County in agricultural pursuits, still its mountain scenery has given it a notoriety, and it is daily becoming a great resort for those who wish to spend a few days or weeks away from the bustle of the city. The town was not incorporated until 1836. Since the completion of the railroad quite a pleasant village has sprung up. The Atlantic & St. Lawrence Railroad Company have erected a large and elegant Hotel known as the Alpine House. The view of the prominent summits of the White Hills from the Station House is intercepted by other small mountains, their base lying almost at the door.

Within an hour's ride are many mountain streams, coursing over the rough stones, and where the worshipers of Isaac Walton can be gratified in either taking out the speckled trout or untangling their lines from the overhanging branches of the trees. Several beautiful curiosities are to be found upon the Androscoggin. Berlin Falls, five miles above the Alpine House, is one of the most beautiful sights to be seen about the mountains. Near the Station House the railroad company have also erected a large machine shop, which gives quite a businesslike appearance to this little village.

Upon leaving Gorham on the west you enter the town of Randolph. In passing through this town you go over the height of land or through the valley lying between the prominent peaks of the White Hills and that portion of the chain called the Pilot Range extending towards the North. In riding over this road you have a view of Mount Monroe,[2] Mount Jefferson, and Adams, which cannot be excelled at any other point, as you pass immediately under them.

Still farther to the west is the town of Jefferson. This town is eighteen miles from Gorham and for mountain scenery is unrivaled. As a township for agricultural purposes it will compare with any town in the county. Through the centre of the town a high ridge of land extends nearly to the westerly boundary. A large Hotel[3] is to be erected at the present season by Mr. H. Plaisted for the accommodation of summer tourists. This location, being upon the northwest of the White Hills, all of the principal mountains are to be seen from their summits to their base, and all the deep ravines and valleys lying upon their northerly side. The Franconia mountains are distinctly seen at this point, Cherry Mountain, the Pilot Range extending some twenty miles to the north, with nearly a quarter of a hundred summits of which this range is composed. This town has for a year or two past been gradually gaining celebrity among the traveling community and will ere long be ranked among the best sites, not only for the grandeur of its scenery, but also for its pure air and healthiness.

To the north of Jefferson and twenty-three miles from the Alpine House is the village of Lancaster. Lancaster is the shire town of the county and is quite a flourishing as well as a pleasant village. It has a commanding view of the Pilot Range, Stratford Peaks, and the large meadows upon the Connecticut river, which is the western boundary of the town. The White Hills are not so distinctly seen at this place, being cut off by other lesser mountains intervening. Mount Prospect, lying in the southerly part of the town, is a round mountain standing alone and commanding as extensive a view as any other mountain north (of) the White Hills. This pretty hill is a pleasant ride of one and a half miles from the village. About two years since, a large and elegant Hotel was erected and since its completion has been well patronized through the summer months.

Whitefield and Dalton located on the westerly side of the Mountains should have a passing notice. They are pleasantly situated within a half-a-day's drive of the White

CHAPTER XIV

———

The manner in which Mr. Crawford lost his
mountain home. Mr. Crawford's death.
The way the children managed to obtain a living.

WE had a few copies of the *History of the White Moun-*
tains printed in 1846 in which Mr. Crawford was
pleased to return his acknowledgements to the public for
their benevolent patronage during our stay there; and as
we expected to return hoped our merit would again render
us the same favors. But it has been overruled against us.

And to make it plain to public minds, and beyond con-
troversy with any who would withhold the truth, I deem it
just to speak names openly; that all may know the reason
why we were deterred from a return to our mountain residence. The men to whom Mr. Crawford gave a claim of his
farm and other property in 1831 were Thomas S. Abbott,
Nathaniel Abbott, and Zera Cutler, all residents of Conway. As our houseroom was limited and there being an
annual increase of visitors, Mr. Crawford was advised to
enlarge his house; this he refused to do under his existing
circumstances, till upon reflection he saw the necessity of
more extensive accommodations and seeing he had never
suffered from debt in which he had been involved since he
first went to the mountains, he also learned that by giving
good sureties and payment of annual interest he could
have the aid of fifteen hundred dollars from the Savings

Bank of Concord. The above named men became sureties for this purpose.

The money obtained by this agency was expended in the needed improvements of our house for the pleasure and comfort of the public. The Abbotts, then employed by the Government for the conveyance of the U. S. Mail from Conway through the Notch of the Mountains to Littleton, were also enabled to carry numerous passengers who were visiting the Mountains; consequently it was of interest to them to have ample accommodations for those who resorted there for mountain scenery. At that time it perhaps resulted in more present profit to them than to us. In consideration of pecuniary aid they could "kill two birds with one stone"; convey the mail and passengers both, making it a profitable enterprize; neither did they for years suffer competition in this successful business. And our intercourse was rendered pleasant and harmonious. At length a series of hardships, heats and colds, incapacitated Mr. Crawford both in body and mentally. Yet a perseverance which marked his life prompted him to look upon the best prospect of things and acquit himself in generosity and justice to all. He suffered almost unremittingly with intense pains, yet he burdened no other ears with the story of his troubles. But his troublesome ills hastened a premature decay of mind and caused him to wander from his native mind more and more rapidly and daily weakened his business faculties. And I, though hourly almost apprized of this sad fact, had a family of little ones who demanded my constant care, and a part of my time must be spent in supplying the comforts of visiting people, by reason of which I was not able to render him the needed assistance in arrangement of his business matters; and strong minded men after doing as much as he had done are not easily persuaded of their irreparable loss of mind and feel reluctant to commit their business to other hands.

It is too often the case that those in whom is reposed the most confidence and who have offered the greatest pretensions to friendship and advice have assumed far different purposes and proved that somewhere there was an intrigue upon money deposits.

In 1837 I was at Guildhall for the benefit of Mr. Crawford's health, and we left my brother upon our mountain farm, and these men having rented it to Mr. Fabyan, Father Crawford refused them possession until they gave him an obligation the summary of which was this: after paying all debts for which they in concurrence with the others had become liable for said Ethan A. Crawford either by signing as sureties or any other manner from the proceeds of the sale of the farm, provided it can be sold for more than enough to pay the amount for which we have signed with him and for him, and the incidental expenses arising from the same, the remainder, if any, after paying such debts and costs, shall go to the wife and children of said Ethan A. Crawford.

August 14th AD 1837

Present	Thomas S. Abbott
Henry Ward	Nathaniel Abbott
Jeremiah Abbott	Zera Cutler

This obligation Father Crawford kept till after our settlement with these men. I have waited many years expecting to redeem our old White Mountain home before I finished my grounded story; I feel that age is following my footsteps very closely, and not knowing when it can be had, my feelings still linger there, and I make no statements

concerning it but what I have means close at hand to cor-
roborate; yet not with a wish to wound the feelings of
any, for I have forgiven them their trespasses in deceiving
me as I expect to be forgiven of mine by my heavenly
Father. I seek no revenge, for God has said, "Vengeance
is *mine* and *I* will repay saith the Lord." I yet live under
the cheering hope of obtaining means to purchase my
mountain home again, whose hallowed recollections and
intimate associations render it dearer to me than Mount
Vernon to those noble ladies whose efforts have been
united in collection of funds to purchase it out of the
hands of speculators.[1]

Mine is now a similar enterprise, hoping by means of
public sympathy and patronage to recall the birthright of
my dear ones from the hands of contending speculation.
The reader perhaps is aware that 1835 was a year of intense excitement in land speculations, and many em-
barked largely in it. Some made a fortune, others lost, while
some were deeply involved in debt. I am here led to speak
of one of these, Thomas S. Abbott, to whom Mr. Crawford
mortgaged his farm. Before Mr. Abbott counted the deep
debt into which he had fallen, the fever of this speculation
abated, and he failed, and made a conveyance of his property to his brother Nathaniel Abbott, sold our mountain
farm with a large tract of wild land Mr. Crawford had obtained from the State (and was called Crawford's Grant)
to one Daniel Burnham in 1842. These men looked over
their account with Mr. Crawford, both debt and credit,
found nearly the sum then due them. The farm they sold
to cover a debt of twelve thousand dollars, as Mr. Burnham told me himself; afterwards sent me the same in his
own handwriting. And before Mr. Burnham got the deed
recorded, Mr. Abbott or his agent put an execution upon

the before named property; then ensued a contention for it, each having an agent, as it was thought best by each to hold no claim themselves. And it has been under legal contention up to the present time.

Mr. Crawford was a man of integrity and trusted largely to the honesty of others in business concerns. In 1844 we were living three-fourths of a mile from our old residence of so many years habitation. Mr. Crawford had an account which had been of fifteen years standing between him and the Abbotts and Cutler, and it had for a long time been my wish for him to obtain a settlement with these men; finally the parties agreed for a settlement with an expressed wish that I should go to Conway with Mr. Crawford. My anxiety for a settlement induced me to go with him and remain among friends while he made a settlement. Mr. Crawford gave them a deed which they called for me to sign, which I did with the express understanding that we should redeem again. They gave us, they said, a good claim, and we should have it again and that without a doubt. Then Mr. Cutler wrote an instrument which I will copy:

> Now we, the said Thomas S. Abbott and Nathaniel Abbott, agree with the said Ethan A. Crawford and his wife Lucy Crawford, that if the title to said farm and the tract of wild land extending on to Mt. Washington shall within two years come into our possession either by purchase or otherwise, that we will sell the same farm and the Davis lot to said Ethan A. Crawford or his wife Lucy Crawford for four thousand dollars and interest from Jan. 24th AD 1842 on receiving the amount in cash or satisfactory Security.   Nov. 30th AD 1844.
>
> Thomas S. Abbott
Nathaniel Abbott

After this was done they wanted to have the matter closed as Mr. Thomas S. Abbott had moved to Portland,

and no further trouble should ensue about this property as there was not a doubt but that this property would fall into their hands before the time expired, and we should have it. Mr. Cutler then made a writing and called upon us to sign it, and by so doing, I and my family of children were cut off from all means of recovering justice.

My friends may be excited with surprise that I should sign that deed and take such a writing for it; and I too but alas! *too late* am led to see the blindness of the movement. But we had dealings with these men since we first made a home at the mountains and placed entire reliance upon them, never thinking they were quietly scheming to wrong us, and it is not so strange a thing after all that we should be so sadly duped, as they said they did not want the place, only what they had paid out for it, and this is all the action they will take upon the matter. One prominent reason why we did not take more extensive precaution to find out all circumstances upon the matter was that Nathaniel Abbott did not want Mr. Burnham to know about our settlement with the expectation of again having the place. But we are led to a query here, if they were just in their motives why it should be kept until it was too late on our part for anything to be done? We were so closely held in these merciless manacles of injustice we were like the reptile under the crushing foot of the sullen serf with not even the power to squirm. We were left destitute of a family refuge.

The fair policy of these men with so many pledges that we should have our home again induced me to sign off from the obligation given to Father Crawford before letting them take possession, from which if I had seasonably foreborne, I might today enjoy the temporal blessing of many thousand dollars. Fearing this continued subject will weary the reader, one circumstance more of these men will at present suffice. They, finding us so passive and trusting their word, thought it best to move on while the tide and current favored them. In Mr. Crawford's settlement with them there was a small amount found due which they did not put in when they sold to Mr. Burnham, which they said should be given in on settlement, and if there is anything more that ought to be allowed to Mr. Crawford that has not been in the settlement, it is to be allowed out of the above balance, and if more, to be paid.

Here a moment's reflection may be cast upon the manner of this settlement with Mr. Crawford. Had it been as he thought and fairly understood it from them, a place would have been left open today for us to have availed ourselves of our rights. They thought as then was the time they would take the advantage of all means that could be used against them;[2] and had a statement of the settlement made from all parties, saying they had made a full and final settlement of all matters between us, dated and signed by each one of us. This sufficiently evinces the fact that they foresaw their favorable result, and that these means were building up the barrier between us and our rights, so fraudulently securing to them our hard earned pittance that neither law nor justice could come to our rescue.

My father formed a settlement in Guildhall, Vermont, at which place I was born in AD 1793, near the banks of the Connecticut river; then the native beauty of the wilderness flourished in the valley and on the mountain top. Among the pleasantest of life's history was when we beheld the opening of the forest and the first spontaneous springing forth of seed scattered over the ashes of the new

slain woodland. In our early cottage of the woods we received counsel by our mother in the temple of the trees,
from the written counsel of God, breathing reverence and
confidence in our hearts, while we drank the *living waters*
of Christ. A mother's precepts and examples upon youth-
ful minds are so indelibly impressed that time's finger can
never wipe them away. We had received the gospel charge
of doing as we would be done by, and it had followed us
through life. I had become a recipient of God's love and
mercy, had learned to trust Him in danger and gloom,
sadness and misfortune. After such admonition of early
days, with the friendly aid of parties in question in former
years, we put that confidence in them that secured all
our property to them. The foregoing reasons are substantially what extended the trust in them to our great
injury. Which having secured to their ends they closed
their hospitality to us, and when asking any assistance
further of them we *knocked* at the gates of *strangers*. Upon
communication with Mr. Cutler to know why he assisted
them against us, he answers, our settlement was fair and
we were satisfied with it; but says nothing of the broken
contract with them that we should have the farm again.
Had this been performed, the pen of such sad history of
their treachery and injustice might have been withheld
from the world today. They triumphed over the gain of
seven thousand dollars which I might have held for my
posterity had I not signed the instrument previously mentioned. So one of the best Portland judges of law told me,
and other good judges have said the same. Some may be
led to enquire why we cherished such a fond regard and
affection for that place. The reader will refer to the commencement of this history which will detail to full satisfaction the motives that first called us there; not for fame

or fortune, but as a kindness to our aged and infirmed parents, whose increasing wants needed kind and tender care. Ethan proved himself a kind and indulgent husband and father, ever watchful of the cares and little troubles of his children either in sickness or health. And we always enjoyed one mind upon common matters.

There seemed to be an adversity to our accumulation of a fortune, although our efforts were great and close in economy to pay all to whom we had become indebted, but made small advancement as one misfortune closely succeeded another, as may be called to mind in the former part of this history. First the fire, which was a loss of three thousand dollars. Yet building almost yearly, with the distance of freighting lumber, always held us behind the times. We had scarcely made up our loss when we were overwhelmed with two floods which beat in pestilence against us, in which we sustained a greater loss than by fire. Mr. Crawford was of such public feeling he would suffer himself to promote public good, and discharged a clear conscience in all his dealings with mankind. . . . [Editor's note: At this point a third of the page has been cut from the manuscript; the next page begins as follows:] even depriving ourselves of the many blessings which others shared for this very purpose. I suffered much in our limited circumstances to give our children the education we desired, though when young we sometimes employed a teacher in our family; and sent them to neighboring schools. And visitors stopping with us rendered them good counsels, by which they gradually acquired good morals and business habits which in the time of destitution rendered [them] not only able to take care of themselves but also to give assistance to the younger ones of the family. In the autumn of 1845 Mr. Crawford was seized with typhoid fever in which he said he should never recover; his fever raged so high we were obliged to keep him in close confinement. Desponding and bewildered spells would come over him, and he then would not be pacified only in the wish to be removed to that home from which we had been outcast and for which we sacrificed all our labor and money. The probability of that mountain home's never being ours again with the prosperity in which we had left it was a great obstacle in the way of his recovery, consequently he was kept too low for medicine to aid him. So constantly did he persist in going home, that we, being unable to prevail against him, finally dressed him, gave him a staff and a man at his side to assist him. He went only a short distance when, his strength failing him, he was glad to return satisfied. His physician told him if he lived through the fever and recovered his health [he] would be as good as in former years. But he would not be convinced of this, and felt that if he did recover from the fever, consumption would follow and close his life. He said he had nothing to live for as our home was taken from us, he had none to go to except the one prepared for him by his Maker. All such ideas I tried to banish from his mind telling him he must not despair of recovering, as he had been the means through God's blessing of bringing a large family into the world, they needed his assistance and counsel in their young and tender years of inexperience. These arguments did not excite or move him to any physical energy; he simply replied that God would "temper the wind to the shorn lamb," and he hoped our children would live to be a comfort to their mother and an honor to their father who would so soon leave them to the mercy of strangers.

[Editor's note: Here follows the passage beginning

"For nearly twenty years we had lived in that secluded and romantic spot" with which Lucy had closed Chapter X in her manuscript and which I have placed at the end of Chapter X in this edition on page 181. In this chapter she continues with an account of her husband's last days.]

Mr. Crawford, living through a long cold winter, we had hopes that he would be again restored to health; yet he never went further away than Littleton but once during the winter, a distance of eighteen miles, but most of the time remained at home with his family whose associations with the society of his children seemed all he wished. Day by day we saw his failure, his desire for nourishment of any kind becoming less and less, some days receiving nothing but a single cracker. From the beginning of his illness death seemed to be foreshadowed to him, and at length we were sorrowfully persuaded it must be so. Upon the twenty-second of June, 1846, his breath grew fainter and shorter until he fell into that slumber from which no obsequious vows or mountain dirges will ever disturb him. No groans or struggles convulsed his frame, but weary with the sorrows and burdens of life he sank away as happy as a careworn laborer sinks to his soft couch of repose. He was we trust received into the praises of the Redeemed and Sanctified. Though never publicly professing religion, he had a very deep respect and love for those whom he thought truly Christian people.

Very soon after the lapse of his illness and death, Mr. William Oakes, a gentleman with whom Mr. Crawford had become familiar, by the many summers they had spent together in scaling the hills and gleaning the valleys for botanical research, came to our bereaved dwelling. He was sadly afflicted because he had not reached us before death had called to dust the head of our family whom he so heartily respected. He poured out his grief in manly tears as he walked the room and thought of the dead. As a tribute of his love he wished the privilege of placing a marble tombstone at his grave in memory of his worth and noble deeds. The next winter he had it prepared and sent to Portland where he wished me to let it remain till he came up the succeeding summer, when he would take it along with him and place it at his grave himself. Mr. Oakes had occasion to go to New Boston previous to the time he designed coming to the Mountains, he bought some articles to take along with him, among which was a quantity of ammunition which he intended to give to the little sportsmen, which he had in his pockets, when he was suddenly sick and stepped to the edge of the boat to vomit, and while in the very act of relieving his stomach he fell overboard, and before he could be recovered he was drowned. Thus perished a generous and noble man. He was educated for the bar but this profession he disliked, and afterwards devoted himself to botany. This was the great satisfaction of his life, to study the different plants, their climate, and their sphere. It was his business for many years. After his sudden death my children had the tombstone brought from Portland and placed at Mr. Crawford's grave with the following inscription prepared by Mr. Oakes.

In memory
of Ethan A. Crawford
Who died June 22nd AD 1846
Aged 54 years
He built here the first hotel at the
White Mountains of which he was for
many years the owner and landlord
he was of great native talent and sagacity
of noble, kind and benevolent disposition,
a beloved husband and father and an
honest and good man

God's ways are unsearchable and past finding out and though mysterious I hope through His blessing some good may ensue from my afflictions. But here I am led to ask what will be the visitations of God's providence upon those who have so seriously wronged us. Experience of years has taught me the frailty of human friends and the need of confiding alone in Him Who remembers in mercy the needs of His children. It had been a trying season with me when under all our burdens, the husband of my youth was gone. I felt then my children must leave me. If I had had no God then unto Whom I could go and Whose mercy I could supplicate, and Whom I could implore to be the Widow's God, and Father of the fatherless, I must have gone down in despair. Yet knowing in Whom I trusted and unto Whom I could go in prayer and faith, believing Him able and willing in His own good time to set the oppressed free, with a clear conscience of injury to none save my own family. And living still with confidence in those with whom we dealt, that when our property fell into their hands, I and my children could repossess their birthright, I felt cheered, and my faltering spirits revived. And when my children left me one after another I commended them to the keeping of Him who gave them, feeling He had power to shield them from every evil and danger, and bless them in life's rough journey.

Under existing circumstances it was thought best by my family to leave the Mountains. A brother[3] of Mr. Crawford's then living at the Mountains, for whom he built a house in 1829 and rendered other aid, when *our* adversity came upon us offered no assistance whatever, therefore I returned to my native state for employment and the advantage of schools for my children. The time had now come when the words of a departed husband seemed to be fully realized, that God would temper the wind to the shorn lamb.

In the summer of 1847 one of my eldest daughters with another lady went to Lowell, Massachusetts, and engaged a tenement in a large brick block which was at that time in building upon the Merrimac corporation.[4] After it was finished they furnished it and entered upon the duties of a boarding house, where they entertained forty female boarders and sometimes even more. A family of our acquaintance occupied the tenement next to my daughter's, who desired to sell and go to California; the furniture was bargained for by my daughter, then another daughter was sent for who bought the household and took possession the following June. Here they lived in close proximity to each other. The first daughter here took a younger sister, the last a sister and brother; and sent them to school and gave them the advantages of music and drawing in all of which they made commendable advancement. This was a pleasant employment, most of the boarders being well bred American ladies, possessed of good morals, attended church regularly upon the Sabbath. They frequently collected together and someone was selected to read for the information of the company. Thus the hours of leisure resulted in much improvement. In those days provisions and labor were very cheap and plenty. All were made happy who were under their charge, and it resulted in a profitable enterprise.

I had two sons younger than my daughters in Lowell, who, having reached the years of manhood, were tired of living as a scattered family. And with the assistance of their sisters bought a handsome situation in a fine growing factory village where we could all live together in useful employment. Here we remained until the most of the children marrying constituted homes of their own; after which we disposed of our situation. Since that time I have a home with them wherever I can be most useful. I believe labor the greatest resource of health, it stimulates the body and has a cheerful tendency upon the mind. These pages will reveal to you the changeable career of my life; the mixture of grief and joy, pleasures and afflictions, through which I have journeyed, wandering from place to place since 1837. My prayer has been and now is that the strife that has been for twenty years existing concerning our mountain home may be ended and myself and family returned to our long loved home.

My Mountain Home

My home! my home, my mountain home, thou'rt dearer
    far to me,
Than any spot in this wide world, how bright so'er it be;
Italia's soft and balmy air, her azure tinted sky,
May from her exiled children claim the tribute of a sigh.
But never can their hearts with deeper feelings glow,
For their own, bright, sunny land, than I on thee bestow.
Erin's green isle is passing fair, her sons are bold and
    true,
But thou art free, my native land, free, fair, and happy,
    too.
O'er thee our bright stars proudly wave, our banner is
    unfurled,
Regardless of oppression's pow'r, fair Eden of the world.
And thou, my own loved mountain home, securely mayst
    thou rest,
A gem of beauty bright and pure, on fair Columbia's
    breast.
Around thy brow the forest pine an emerald wreath has
    made,
While sunbeams circle round thy head, and gild thy
    deepest glade.
I love thee well, my mountain home, my heart is still
    with thee,
With all things bright and beautiful, with all things glad
    and free;
They steal upon my spirit now, bright visions of the past;
Oh let them fall upon my soul, while time for me shall last.

The home so fondly cherished now presents a melancholy appearance. The pastures have grown to bushes, the meadows so sadly neglected present to view nothing but a cold damp moss intermixed with strawberry vines and scattering grass, the house swept to desolation in a conflagration while Mr. Fabyan occupied it.[5] Since then a work of incendiary was committed upon the barns in the nighttime, the fire being discovered by Mr. Brabrooks who lived three-quarters of a mile distant, he and a neighbor on arriving there in the morning discovered the track of a horse and wagon and the place where the horse was tied, then turned back towards Carroll; they however having no interest did not follow to ascertain the rogue, and I am unable to say whether he has since been detected. There, the place once so lovely and lively a resort for rural visitors, now lies a sad and deplorable ruin. There have been since several houses built for mountain company so the need of this will be scarcely missed; yet I think perchance someone in passing by or viewing it from the summit of Mount Washington will cast a tribute of sympathy upon me who has surrendered it to such a fate. There it lies an unprofitable barren waste affording only a subject of contention and plea for jurists. When all else shall fail me I can adopt the following as a surviving consolation.

> God of my childhood and my youth,
> The guide of all my days,
> I have declared thy heavenly truth,
> And told thy wonderous ways.
>
> Wilt thou forsake my hoary hairs,
> And leave my fainting heart?
> Who shall sustain my sinking years
> If God, my strength depart?

Let me thy power and truth proclaim,
To the surviving age;
And leave a savour of thy name
When I shall quit the stage.

The land of silence and of death,
Attend my next remove,
O may these poor remains of breath
Teach the wide world Thy love.

Finis

NOTES

CHAPTER I

1 This is one of the few places in which the manuscript of 1860 is more specific than the book. I have therefore substituted it for the sentence in Chapter IV of the book which reads as follows: "This summer there came a considerable large party of distinguished characters, such as the author of the New Hampshire map, etc., to my house, about noon, to ascend the mountains and give names to such hills as were un-named, and after a dinner of trout, they set out, taking me for a guide and baggage-carrier."

2 Blue Pond is the Lakes of the Clouds. It was also later called Washington's Punch Bowl. F. Allen Burt, *The Story of Mount Washington* (Hanover, N. H., 1960), p. 23.

CHAPTER II

1 In the book this is Chapter I.

2 This is an example of Lucy Crawford's occasionally shaky syntax.

3 Uncupy, or spirit—obviously an Indian word; it is capitalized in the edition of 1846 and in the manuscript, which is more explicit: "Uncupy (rum)."

4 Lucy Crawford's manuscript has this variant: "There was not that distinction in dress, which so far at the present day keeps many a hard working man in poverty."

5 In the manuscript "meditation" is crossed out and "watch" written over it.

6 At this point in the manuscript Lucy Crawford has related the episodes about Nash and Sawyer and the gentleman and his wife who met a moose while travelling towards the Notch which in the book occur at the end of Chapter X and which will be found in this edition on pp. 175, 177. At the bottom of the page in the manuscript Lucy has written: "Here insert the plate representing the moose

jumping over the horse and sleigh." The plate, alas, has not been included in the manuscript.

CHAPTER III

1 In the book this is Chapter II.

2 The manuscript has: "At the age of 20, in 1812, Ethan enlisted etc."

3 The manuscript has: "In 1814, Ethan went into the state of New York and let himself to work, taking out trees by the roots" etc. The manuscript account of Ethan's New York experience follows substantially the account in the book except for the interpolation of this passage: "Mr. Crawford was a verry stout athletic man, standing six feet and two inches (not seven feet, as Mr. Willey has it in his work) in his stockings. We think none of the boys of Mr. Abel Crawford (the old Patriarch, so called) were less than six feet in height, and from that six feet three inches."

CHAPTER IV

1 In the book this is Chapter III.

2 In the book this is the first paragraph of Chapter IV.

3 This brass plate was stolen by a party of vandals from Jackson, celebrating the Glorious Fourth, in 1825. Burt, *op. cit.*, p. 20. See p. 74.

4 The manuscript puts it this way: "The Notch road was fast becoming the great thoroughfare between Northern New Hampshire, Vermont, and the towns upon the eastern coast. Most of the produce, pork, etc. was carried over this road in two and one horse sleighs, which brought a considerable amount of custom to the Notch House during the winter season. A string of two horse pungs (so called) of a quarter to a half a mile in length was no uncommon occurrence in those days."

5 This was the beginning of the Crawford Path.

6 The manuscript gives this description of the traps: "These traps are formed by a lever power, so constructed that when the gate is touched the lever falls upon the animal and kills or holds him."

7 Approximately the present road from Fabyan's to the Base Station.

8   According to the manuscript it was at this point Ethan fainted: "The blood had stopped and Ethan differed with her in opinion, he thinking that it would heal quicker by not disturbing it. The old lady still insisted that it was necessary and proceeded to unbandage the ancle, when the blood again began to flow more freely, which caused the mountain giant to faint."

CHAPTER V

1   This chapter is Chapter V and part of Chapter VI in the book.

2   In the manuscript Lucy Crawford has added a descriptive passage: "The ladies returned much gratified, having ascended to that height which caused the country round about to appear like [a] map at their feet. An endless number of small streams are to be seen winding their course down the different valleys untill they find their way into the Connecticut and Merrimack upon the west and southerly side of the mountains and into the Androscoggin upon the north and east. The prospect from the summit is boundless, and the variety of scenery so great as to chain the eye upon the different objects, hour after hour."

3   In the manuscript: "Ethan, who considered bears as mere playthings, calmed down his fears. . ."

4   James Kent (1763-1847), Chief Justice of the New York Supreme Court, Chancellor of the New York Court of Chancery, author of *Commentaries on American Law*. This paragraph is the beginning of Chapter VI in the book, but is omitted from the manuscript.

5   Lucy Crawford, too, was impressed by her husband's prowess with the horn, which she mentions in several places in her manuscript, as in this tribute following the reference to the lady's "feelings": "It required the stentorian lungs of Ethan Allen Crawford to shake the mountain's sides with this monster horn."

6   The episode in this paragraph is omitted from the manuscript. Instead Lucy Crawford brings forward the episode of the lost gentleman to be found in this edition on page 55, with the lesson "never to give up a certainty for an uncertainty". This makes a rather better ending to the chapter than the present ending; indeed it is the ending of Chapter V in the original edition, as well as in her manuscript. In spite of the abruptness of the transition be-

tween Chapters V and VI, it has seemed best in this, as in most cases, to follow the order of the book rather than that of Lucy's manuscript. The sentence about thunder showers from the manuscript, which opens the next chapter, makes the transition somewhat less abrupt.

CHAPTER VI

1 In the manuscript this is followed by the following paragraph of description:

"A storm upon tip-top is awful and terrifick. The clouds fly past you almost with lightning speed, and so dense that an object cannot be seen scarcely the length of a rod. It seems to fill the mind with awe, as one sits under the covering of the "Tip-Top Houses, and beholds the storm raging without. It appears, in witnessing a rain storm at this height, more like the blustering snow storms of February."

(This passage is a good illustration of the inconsistencies in the manuscript.)

2 The manuscript has this variant of the last two sentences of this paragraph: "This was the last of these species of animals that Mr. Crawford ever saw while living about the mountains. He had made such havoc among them, that season, that he either destroyed the race or drove them from that region of the country."

3 In the manuscript this reads: "During the month of October, 1825". Here her memory has failed her. It is obvious from the context—the reference to "the winter of 1824" on the next page—that this was October, 1823. See note 5 below.

4 This "Notch House" (which is also referred to on page 41) is not the Notch House at the head of the Notch, built by Ethan and Abel Crawford in 1828, but the "Old Notch House", built by a Mr. Davis in 1793; hired by Ethan Allen Crawford in "this fall" of 1823; occupied by the Willey family in October, 1825; and spared by the slide of 1826. See Burt, *op. cit.*, pp. 32, 41.

5 At this point Chapter VI of the manuscript ends. But it has been preceded by a long passage in which Lucy Crawford goes into the reasons for the additions made in their house in 1824. Though there is some repetition of the paragraph beginning "The winter of 1824" I quote the whole passage:

"It was evident, beyond doubt, that if the summer travell increased as it had for a few years past, that the Crawford house could not accomodate them all. As the lumber must all be drawn a distance of twelve miles, it became necessary to start early in the winter to draw it, if he made any addition to his buildings. Most of the winter of 1824 was thus spent in making preparations and getting the lumber home. The next spring an addition was made to the house thirty six by forty feet, two stories high. Mr. Crawford's means being quite limited, the house was not entirely finished until the next season, although it served to shelter those whose curiosity had brought them to the mountains. The summer of 1825 was principally engaged by Ethan in acting as guide up the mountains, to the numerous visiters, who only considered themselves safe under his protection. If a lady became weary or fatigued, so as to be unable to proceed, she was mounted upon the shoulders of the 'mountain giant' and safly carried home. Among the number who came this season, was a landscape painter, who took several beautiful sketches. The winter travel was increasing nearly in same ratio with the summer. Portland, Me., and Portsmouth, N. H., were fast drawing the business from all the country north and west of the mountains for a considerable distance. The road was being yearly improved, although the winds were severe and piercing through the notch to the teamsters. Ethan A. Crawford house was a general resort to that class of travellers, owing not entirely to the location, which was a sort of half-way-place through the Notch, but from the fact that it was more of a teamsters home. Ethan was always ready to receive them, and during the long winter evenings he entertained them with the marvelous connected with and about the mountains."

CHAPTER VII

1   The summer of 1824. The beginning of Chapter VII of the manuscript corresponds to the beginning of Chapter VII in the book.

2   Lucy Crawford in the manuscript is more explicit: "This, [the marquee] with a sheet iron stove, he packed in as small compass as possible, (which weighed over eighty pounds) he started off for the summit of Mt. Washington, with the pack upon his back. Any person can well imagine, who has climbed over the present im-

proved roads, what strength it would require to carry a load of nearly an hundred weigh[t] up the mountain over the route of those days."

As to the "athletic and robust man" who "kindly volunteered his services to shoulder the pack", she has this to say: "Ethan placed it firmly upon his back, so as to ride without rolling from side to side, as it requires skill in packing as well as in all other business, but they had not proceeded but a short distance up the hill, before he quietly lay down his load to rest. Ethan laughingly picked it up, strapped it again upon his own shoulders and conveyed it the remainder of the way."

3   In the manuscript Lucy Crawford gives this direction:
"To the Printer
All quotations to be set in Brevier type solid"
This quotation and the other quotations from the album in this chapter have been cut from the edition of 1846 and pasted on the sheets of the manuscript.

4   Probably William Oakes (1799-1848), author of *Scenery of the White Mountains*, published in 1848. He visited the White Mountains with his friend Dr. Charles Pickering in 1825 and 1826 and every summer from 1843 until his death. Kilbourne, *op. cit.*, pp. 37, 38. Burt, *op. cit.*, p. 187.

5   Apparently Lucy Crawford's first trip to the summit.

6   The crag from which the trestle on the cog railway takes its name.

7   In the book Chapter VII ends here.

8   In the manuscript this sentence reads: "When they wished to retire, a blanket was drawn in front of their camp, and they were left entirely by themselves, to be sung to sleep by the untiring musquitoe."

CHAPTER VIII

1   I have substituted this paragraph from Lucy Crawford's manuscript for the following paragraph in the edition of 1846:

"I never knew a single person that ever took cold from these wild excursions. We frequently received letters from invalids saying their healths were much improved by this visit with us."

Here she has expanded a passage rather than condense it, as is her usual practice.

2 This paragraph, which makes an abrupt transition in both the edition of 1846 and Lucy Crawford's manuscript, is condensed in the manuscript to two sentences, the first giving the dimensions of the new stables followed by this sentence of explanation: "There being no railroad facilities, as at the present day, to convey people from one part of the country to another, those who visited the mountains, for the most part, came in their own private carriages, which required a great amount of stable room."

3 "Sat down", the manuscript reads, "around the fire, in imitation of Indians, to listen to the stories of Ethan, whose list never run out, of the hair-breadth escapes, &c of his mountain life, until they lay down to rest for the night."

4 In the manuscript the rest of this sentence reads: "for so young a girl, and was a favorite with all who became aquainted with her pleasing address and good humer."

5 The manuscript adds: "It was somewhat singular, that they should leave the only spot that remained untouched for the space of miles; the magnitude of this slide was far greater than most persons are aware of; its length was nearly three miles, and extending to the top of the mountains. The most probable supposition is, that they remained in the house, (the children in beds, as the beds were found without being made up,) until nearly the whole slide had passed by, as the bodies were not buried to verry great depth. It has been supposed by some, that they remained until that portion of the shed and barn was struck and fell in, when fear drove them from their home. Others have thought that they were all together at the place which Mr. Willey had selected for a refuge of safety."

6 The manuscript, however, does add this passage: "A family of nine person[s], all in good health, and enjoying all the pleasures that a mountain life affords, causing the hill sides to echo back their merry peals of laughter, were, thus in a twinkling of an eye, as it were, launched into eternity. The funeral was attended by the Elder Samuel Hasaltine, then living in the town of Bartlett. He was a particular friend of the Willey family, and his prayer was well adapted to the occasion. More appropriate language or more impressive, could not have been used, than that which he quoted from Isaiah, at the commencement of his services, viz:—"Who hath measured the waters in the hollow of his hand, and meted out heaven with a span, and comprehended the dust of the earth in a measure, and weighed the mountains in scales, and the hills in a balance.""

7 Lucy Crawford's language is more forthright: "Some of the occupants of the Willey house, since that time, worse than brutes, tore it down and used it for fuel."

CHAPTER IX

1 At this point the chapter headings of book and manuscript correspond.

2 It was on his visit to the mountains in September, 1832 that Hawthorne heard this story from Ethan Allen Crawford, as well as the account of the Willey family. The visit resulted in a sketch, "Our Evening Party among the Mountains", and two tales, "The Great Carbuncle" and "The Ambitious Guest". Kilbourne, *op. cit.*, pp. 115-116.

3 The manuscript introduces the story of Nancy with the following descriptive passage: "It will be recollected by those who have visited this spot, that the stream so called, as 'Nancy's Brook', is about one-half of a mile below the Mt. Crawford House, taking its rise far up the mountain, tumbling its waters over large precipices as it decends down through the heavy forests below. But few small streams so readily attract the attention of the traveller as this; time has suffered this stream to cut out deep channels varying from ten to thirty feet, giving the appearance of flumes. It is by nature a wild spot, and taken in connection with the death of Nancy, the eye naturally rests upon the scene."

4 From this point the manuscript departs somewhat from the account in the book; Lucy Crawford having manifestly been moved by Nancy's story, goes into more detail about her:

"With a small bundle under her arm, wet and fatigued by the long walk from Lancaster, she set out upon her perilous undertaking. The drifting snow driven by a cold northwest wind rendered her progress slow. She however succeeded in reaching the Notch but too late to find the object of her affections there." An abbreviated account of the burnt-out fire follows. The manuscript proceeds: "The disappointment of not meeting the men at this place did not discourage her. After warming herself she again started down through the Notch, but having taken no provisions with her she soon began to feel the need thereof. In passing over the stream since known as 'Nancy's Brook' the bottom of her cloths became exceeding wet, and with hunger and fatigue she halted upon its banks, under the branches of an old tree. When Nancy left the farm of Col. Whipple's, the family who had tried to persuade her not to follow the men through the dark forest, had not the least idea that she would penetrate far into the woods in so blustering a night, but would soon return to the farm. But as the evening wore away and she did not return, a feeling of anxiety soon disturbed the family circle. The male portion, after consulting, concluded to go out and persuade her to give up the idea of any farther pursuing.''

They find the fire and eventually "poor Nancy . . . frozen to death". The poem is omitted, but Lucy makes this comment: "We think her treacherous deceiver did not long live to be censured with thought of murdering the one who had placed confidence in him and looked to him as a protector, but as a just reward his reason was deprived him, and he soon after died in a mad house, a raving maniac. Various reports have gone forth since the above sad occurance, of strange noises being heard about the spot where she was found, but like most of the ghost stories, they have been found to proceed from screech owls, who live in this secluded spot undisturb.''

5 In the book this is the first sentence of Chapter X. In the manuscript we are still in Chapter IX. Not only that but with a slight variation—"In October of the following fall there came etc."—this sentence directly follows the "undisturb" of the quotation in the note above. Perhaps Lucy, who is generally careful about her paragraphing, was unduly "disturb" by Nancy's pathetic story.

6 ". . . blowing the horn." In the manuscript this is followed by "producing such a sound as no other man was ever able to make". And Lucy adds a further tribute to Ethan's horn-blowing prowess later in the paragraph: "and when the sound of the horn greeted their ears no music ever sounded sweeter. 'Home, sweet home', played from the parlor, upon a piano, by the delicate fingers of a female, never brought Home so near as did that old six feet Tin mountain horn, to a lost traveller.''

7 i.e., the road toward the base of Mount Washington.

8 The manuscript adds "four miles below his Ethan's settlement." This, of course, is the Notch House, on the site of the present Crawford House, built by Ethan and Abel Crawford in 1828, in which Ethan's brother, Thomas J. was installed as manager in 1829 as related on page 111.

9 The manuscript puts this "with the staff in his own hands."

10 Tuckerman's Ravine. The passage recounts the discovery of

the famous "Snow Arch". One of the botanists was Dr. James W. Robbins of Uxbridge, Massachusetts (he was a friend of William Oakes) who visited the mountains in July, 1829. Burt, *op. cit.*, pp. 187-188.

11 Lucy adds: "Trapping with Ethan became a second nature; it was as much of a luxury to him to entrap a wild animal as it ever was to a native son of the forest."

12 More accurately one of the sources of the east branch of the Pemigewasset River. Called "Ethan's Pond"—on the Crawford Notch quadrangle, "Ethan Pond".

13 Chapter IX of the manuscript ends with this sentence.

CHAPTER X

1 The table of contents is incomplete for this chapter in the manuscript. For after the passage on "mountain echoes" on pages 132-133 the manuscript account continues with many personal details about the Crawford family. In the book there are more details about family illnesses, financial difficulties, etc. which Lucy did not include in the manuscript. In the book Chapter X runs to approximately ninety pages; about twenty-five of these pages have been included in Chapter IX in this text. Note the change from the third person of the manuscript in the introductory paragraph to the first person of the book in the second.

2 In the manuscript Lucy not only paraphrases this passage but also, as she does occasionally, elaborates upon it. After explaining how deer "are as fond of salt as the horned cattle in our barnyard", she proceeds to tell how the young man "set out in good cheer and arriving at the place, being ambitious to get a shot at an animal which he had never yet seen wild in the forest, he approached with great care, following his instructions from Mr. Crawford closely soon had the gratification to see a noble deer trot along up to the log and commence lapping the hollow, for the salt was eaten up and dissolved by the falling rain. After taking a view of his intended prize, he silently drew his gun to his shoulder and fired. The deer had received the contents in his head and fell, the young man then springing upon him, severed his jugular and with the assistance of another person returned in triumph to the house."

3 Lucy says that the others took the same method as "the old Patriarch" but "after witnessing the elder Crawford's feat, suffered

themselves not to proceed so rapidly, by means of a staff in their hands."

4 This account of Ethan's troubles with "the man from Jefferson" (pp. 135-138) is omitted from the manuscript.

5 This quotation from the Crawford House album is copied in longhand in the manuscript, but the "poetic effusion" and the paragraph which follows it have been cut from the edition of 1846 and pasted to the sheet with a notation for the printer for each passage: "Burgeois type, solid".

6 The account of Lucy's illness and the disposition of the child (pp. 147-148) is not in the manuscript.

7 This account of Ethan's illness is abridged in the manuscript to the following paragraph:

"Mr. Crawford, from the many losses he had met with by floods and fires, had become considerably involved, and as his health was beginning to fail, he concluded to sell out his interest at the mountains, supposing it would be a relief to his mind, and perhaps be beneficial to his family, as their means of attending school while living in the secluded spot was rather limited."

8 At this point Lucy summarizes the next two pages in the following passage:

"Before this bond expired, the excitement which had been prevailing to so great an extent, abated, and a reaction followed, rendering it almost impossible to dispose of real estate at any price. As the health of Mr. Crawford was poor, and no opportunity offering by which he could sell his farm and buildings, his creditors became uneasy, and soon began to force him up to payments, until he turned out his personal property down to his last cow, his real estate soon to pass from him by mortgage. The elder children of Ethan were fast approaching manhood and began to show symptoms of having inherited some of his peculiarities, particularly those strong desires for hunting and fishing. The winter of 1836 . . . ."

There follows the account of the deer hunting on page 154 ff.

9 The account of the deer hunting stops at this point. The various vicissitudes of the Crawford family given in pages 157 to 165 are omitted from the manuscript except for two paragraphs of summary with which Chapter X of the manuscript ends. I have placed these paragraphs at the end of Chapter X in this text.

10 Dr. Samuel A. Bemis, a Boston dentist, who spent his summers from 1827 to 1840 in Hart's Location, where Abel Crawford

kept the Mount Crawford House. He built and made his home in the stone house known as Notchland until his death in 1881. Kilbourne, *op. cit.*, p. 137.

11   Abel Crawford died in 1851 at the age of eighty-five.

12   Davis managed the Mount Crawford House for his father-in-law and in the eighteen-forties built the third bridle path up Mount Washington, still known as the Davis Path. Burt, *op. cit.*, p. 50.

13   This account of the Lovewell Massacre is taken from Chapter XIII of the manuscript.

14   The Nash and Sawyer episode and the account of the man and his wife who met the moose on page 177 were given in the manuscript in Chapter II. See note 6 to that chapter.

CHAPTER XI

1   This sentence is an example of Lucy Crawford's occasional lapse from strict grammatical virtue.

2   Kilbourne—*op. cit.*, p. 53—gives the Indian name as Singrawack, said to mean "The Foaming Stream of the White Rock".

3   Here Lucy Crawford's geography appears to be at fault; the bogs and ponds around Whitefield, northwest of Cherry Mountain, seem to be the source of John's River.

4   She has snipped this passage from Spaulding's book and pasted it to the manuscript sheets. In doing so she has omitted an introductory sentence: "A description of another wonderful escape is found in Rev. H. White's *History of New England*, p. 327." This omission explains the otherwise mysterious quotation marks in the passage in the text.

CHAPTER XII

1   Frederick Strickland, son of Sir George Strickland, M. P. of Bridlington, England. Burt, *op. cit.*, pp. 127, 128.

2   The plural is correct for the time when Lucy Crawford was writing—1860. The first summit house was built by Joseph S. Hall in 1852. The Tip Top House—of stone—was built in 1853; it is the only one of the nineteenth century buildings built on the summit which still stands. Burt, *op. cit.*, pp. 66, 67.

3 Two pages later she spells this name Braybrook. Burt, *op. cit.*, refers to "Brabrook's White Mountain House".

4 J. L. Gibb had recently taken over the hotel at the head of the Notch from Thomas J. Crawford, Kilbourne, *op. cit.*, pp. 162, 163.

5 The neighboring ridge is called Chandler Ridge in his memory.

6 Colonel Joseph M. Thompson. Burt, *op. cit.*, p. 56. A more complete account of the ownership and operation of the Summit Houses at this time may be found in Burt, Chapter 5.

7 This sentence is a paraphrase of the account in Spaulding's *Historical Relics of the White Mountains* upon which Lucy Crawford relied for much of the material in this chapter. (John H. Spaulding, Boston, 1855.) Kilbourne, *op. cit.*, pp. 218, 219.

8 Now known as the Great Gulf, more accurately between Mount Washington and Mount Jefferson.

9 Again Lucy Crawford's geography is at fault. The lake in Tuckerman's Ravine is Hermit Lake; Spaulding's Lake is in the Great Gulf.

10 Lucy Crawford is referring either to the Profile House, just north of the Old Man of the Mountains, which was opened in 1853, or perhaps to the Mount Lafayette House, burned in 1861, situated two miles and a half below the Profile House. Kilbourne, *op. cit.*, pp. 168, 169.

11 This boulder was swept away by an avalanche on June 20, 1883. Kilbourne, *op. cit.*, p. 303.

CHAPTER XIII

1 Opened from Montreal to Portland in July, 1853 and leased for 999 years in the same year to the Grand Trunk Railway, and known since as the Grand Trunk. Kilbourne, *op. cit.*, p. 221.

2 This should, of course, be Mount Madison, Mount Monroe being southwest of Mount Washington. The proper order is: Mount Madison, Mount Adams, Mount Jefferson.

3 Probably the present Waumbeck: a hotel was built at about this time and later remodelled. Kilbourne, *op. cit.*, p. 342.

CHAPTER XIV

1 Lucy refers to the Ladies Mount Vernon Association which acquired possession of Mount Vernon in 1858.

2 This clause is somewhat ambiguous; does Lucy perhaps mean against "*us*" rather than against "them"?

3 "A brother"—that is, Thomas J. Crawford.

4 The Merrimack Manufacturing Company, the first of the textile industries which were to make Lowell famous, was incorporated in 1822. Later the company built the boarding houses for its female operatives, largely drawn from the rural areas of New England, whose condition won the admiration of Dickens in his visit to the United States in 1842 and as late as 1861 led Anthony Trollope to describe Lowell as "the realization of a commercial Utopia".

5 The old Crawford inn burned in 1853. It had been renamed by Horace Fabyan "The Mount Washington House". Kilbourne, *op. cit.*, pp. 164, 165.

APPENDIX

———

CRAWFORDS AND ROSEBROOKS

THE close association of the Crawfords and the Rosebrooks is evident from Lucy Crawford's account.
What she does not tell us is that the two families were
acquainted with each other before they came to the North
Country. She mentions the fact, in her account of the
Rosebrooks, that Hannah Hanes of Brimfield, Massachusetts married Eleazar Rosebrook of Grafton, which is
twenty-five miles or so to the northeast. But Brimfield is
only ten miles or so north of Union, Connecticut, which
is Crawford territory.

For Fred E. Crawford, in his biography of his father
Oramel (privately printed, 1952), tells us that James
Crawford, the progenitor of the Guildhall branch of the
family, was born in Ulster, Ireland and came to Boston in
1726, moved from Newton, Massachusetts to Union, Connecticut around 1740 and lived there thirty years. His
third son John, born in Boston in 1734, married, in 1757,
Mary Rosebrook, who was the sister of Eleazar. John and
Mary Rosebrook Crawford, the biography further relates,
began their trek northward in 1779, moving from Union,
Connecticut to Grassy Brook, later Brookline, near West-
minster, Vermont. Nor did the family stop there. Of their
eleven children several of the sons moved up the Connecticut River finally settling in and around Guildhall,
Vermont.

One of them, John, Jr., in 1792 bought a farm in

Guildhall. (This later descended to his son, Oramel, whose son Fred E. Crawford wrote the above-mentioned biography; known as the Old Home Crawford, it is now owned by Frederick C. Crawford, John, Jr.'s great-grandson.) On their son's farm John and Mary Rosebrook Crawford spent their last years and here John died in 1817—the same year in which Ethan and Lucy's other grandfather Rosebrook died in Carroll, New Hampshire, as Lucy relates.

Eleazar Rosebrook and his wife Hannah Hanes Rosebrook had seven children. The Rosebrooks had also moved northward; their second daughter, Hannah, was born in Lancaster, New Hampshire, October 30, 1773; and she married Abel Crawford, another son of John and Mary Rosebrook Crawford, who had moved to Guildhall; these were the parents of Ethan Allen Crawford. The Rosebrooks' oldest daughter, Mercy, born in Union, Connecticut, September 7, 1772, married Samuel Howe, also of Guildhall; they were the parents of Lucy. Thus Ethan and Lucy were first cousins, to say nothing of their connection through Ethan's grandparents, John and Mary Rosebrook Crawford.

Abel Crawford, born in 1766, moved from Guildhall to the Giant's Grave in 1791, as related by F. Allen Burt, in *The Story of Mount Washington*, and brought his wife Hannah and two sons Erastus and Ethan Allen there the next year. Shortly thereafter his father-in-law, Eleazar Rosebrook, bought him out and he moved down the Notch into Hart's Location, where he later built the Mount Crawford House and spent the rest of his life, dying in his eighty-fifth year in 1851. In 1845, as Ethan relates in Chapter X, his mother, in her seventy-fourth year, was "enjoying tolerably good health, after having raised a family of nine children."

Eleazar Rosebrook, nursed by his granddaughter Lucy, as she relates, died of cancer in 1817. Hannah Hanes Rosebrook outlived him by several years, dying at the age of eighty-four on May 4, 1829.

THEIR BURYING GROUND

It is fitting that Ethan and Lucy and their grandparents, the Rosebrooks, who together with Abel Crawford, the Patriarch, and his wife Hannah Rosebrook, were the pioneers of the Crawford Country, should be buried in a family burying ground. This is located on a slight rise three-tenths of a mile from Route 302 on the highway to the base of the mountain which was Ethan's bailiwick. It is not visible from the highway but may be reached in a two minutes' walk by a track into the woodland.

It is a plot about twenty-five feet square. The fence in the photograph facing page 105 has been replaced by iron pipes sunk into eight sturdy granite posts. At the front of the plot is the resting place of the Rosebrooks, marked by two slate stones with arched tops: columns are lightly etched upon the sides of the stones, and urns of differing design are etched upon the spaces below the arches. The inscriptions on the stones are finely chiselled: Eleazar's reads:

> In memory of
> Cap. Eliezer Rosebrook
> who died Sep. 25
> 1817
> in the 70 year
> of his age

> When I lie buried deep in dust,
> My flesh shall be thy care;
> These with'ring limbs with thee I trust,
> To raise them strong and fair.

His wife's reads:

> Widow
> Hannah Rosebrook
> died May 4th
> 1829
> age 84

> Blessed are the dead who die in
> the Lord, for they rest from their
> labors and their works do follow
> them.

To the right of these graves is the granite shaft, seen in the foreground of the photograph, which was erected to Ethan and Lucy after the latter's death. The inscriptions read:

> Ethan A
> Crawford
> died
> June 22, 1846
> Ae. 52 yrs.

> Lucy
> His wife
> Died Feb. 17, 1869
> Ae. 76 yrs.

Behind the granite shaft on the other side of the lot is the simple marble stone which William Oakes provided after Ethan's death, as related in Chapter XIV. The inscription reads:

> In Memory of
> Ethan Allen Crawford
> who died
> June 22, A.D. 1846
> Aged 52

There follow the lines which Lucy quotes in her last chapter. On both monuments Ethan's age is incorrectly given as fifty-two. Since he was born in 1792 the correct age should, of course, be fifty-four as, in fact, it is given in Lucy's manuscript.

Behind the marble tombstone are two low headstones marked on the top: FATHER MOTHER. Beside Ethan's stone and Eleazar's are two flag holders placed there by GAR Post 55; for both were soldiers, Ethan as a corporal in the War of 1812, as related in Chapter III of this edition; Eleazar Rosebrook in the Revolution. Norway pines surround the plot, blocking out the view of the mountains visible in the photograph facing page 105. The plot and the mound on which it is situated are carpeted with soft green moss. Appropriately the sound of the unseen cars passing on the highway below comes muted to this last resting place of these intrepid pioneers.

INDEX